Designing with KANJI

"Love"

Japanese Character Motifs
for Surface, Skin & Spirit

Shogo Oketani & Leza Lowitz

Published by
Stone Bridge Press LLC, P. O. Box 8208, Berkeley, CA 94707
TEL 510-524-8732 • sbp@stonebridge.com • www.stonebridge.com

Text © 2003 Shogo Oketani and Leza Lowitz.

Book design by L. J. C. Shimoda (www.shimodaworks.com).
Kanji examples on page 8 by H. E. Davey (www.senninfoundation.com).

Printed in the United States of America.

8 7 6 5 4 3   2006 2007 2008 2009 2010

ISBN 1-880656-79-5 (978-1-880656-79-2)

Contents

Introduction

From "Wife" to "Wind God"

Over the last several years, *kanji*—Japanese characters, also called "ideograms" or "pictograms"—have made their way into the Western mind, onto the body, and just about everywhere else. Just as Japanese like to use English words and expressions on T-shirts, caps, signage, and ads, often with unintentionally humorous results, Westerners now adorn their flesh, clothes, and designs with kanji, sometimes with similar, mistaken outcomes.

Once, when we were watching TV in Tokyo, we turned on a talk show and saw a perfect example. A young Japanese woman had gone to a downtown bar, where she met an attractive American man. Striking up a conversation, he told her that he'd been interested in Japanese culture since he was a teenager. He said he even had the kanji for "Wind God" tattooed on his arm. In Japanese, "Wind God" is *fūjin* and the kanji for it is 風神. He rolled up his sleeve and showed it to her.

Unfortunately for him, the tattoo was not "Wind God" but "Wife" (夫人), which is pronounced *fujin* (that is, with a short *u*). Obviously, the tattoo parlor had mistakenly chosen the kanji characters based on their similar pronunciation.

When the Japanese woman saw the man's tattoo, she felt too embarrassed to tell him the truth. So she smiled and told him how nice it was. Then she pretended to have another appointment and left the bar. He might still be wondering why Japanese women don't like the "Wind God."

The Origin of Kanji

The word "kanji" is the Japanese pronunciation of the Chinese word *hanzi*, which means "Chinese ideogram." The ideograms for "kanji" are 漢字. The kanji 漢 means "the Han people" (the majority race in China), and 字 means "letters." The original meaning of "kanji" is thus "letters used by the Han people."

Kanji are currently the only extant ideographic characters used in the world. Kanji originated from hieroglyphics carved on animal bones and turtle shells during the Yin dynasty, around 1600 B.C. Turtle shells were placed in a fire, and the future was foretold by reading the cracks produced by the heat. Over three thousand of these documents of divination were found in the 1890s in Hepei, China.

By the time of the fall of the Yin dynasty around 1000 B.C., many books, including the first Chinese poetry collection *Sihjing* (詩経), were being written with ideograms. The style of ideograms seen today was established in A.D. 200, although there have been many evolutions in meaning since then, along with a general trend toward simplifying the forms of the characters. Today, there are over thirty thousand kanji accepted for use in China. In Japan the number is much lower: some two thousand for everyday use in newspapers and ordinary reading matter and perhaps another several thousand to accommodate specialists, scholars, and historians.

Beauty and Meaning

Kanji are incredibly beautiful and creative. They represent meaning in a visually expressive way, often mirroring the shapes of the things they describe.

For example, the kanji for "hand" 手 and "eye" 目 both look like the things they represent. The five digits of the hand are reflected in the lines of the kanji for "hand," and the pupil and whites are represented in the kanji for "eye."

手: ᗰᗰ ᖴ ᖴ ᖴ 手   目: ◁ ᗧ ᗧ ◁ 目 目

Yet some kanji don't look at all like the thing they signify. Rather, they form a chain of meaning by association. Let's take the kanji 計 as an example. It means "to count." This kanji is made of 言, which means "to say," and 十, which means "ten." It literally means "to say numbers from one to ten," or simply, "to measure or count."

Some kanji can express both meaning and pronunciation and were created in cases where there were homonyms. For example, let's look at the following three kanji, which are pronounced *pi* or *bi* in Chinese.

皮 (*pi*): "skin "
彼 (*bi*): "that," or "distant" as in "that side"
疲 (*pi*): "tired"

At first glance, you can see that each of these three kanji contains the component 皮. This kanji by itself meant "to flay an animal": hence, "skin." In ancient Chinese the words for "skin," "that," and "tired" were homonyms; each was pronounced *pi* or *bi*. So different kanji needed to be created to distinguish their meanings.

The first kanji was 皮 or "skin." This kanji can stand alone. "That" or "distant" was then made by adding 彳, the component for "going": 彼.

"Tired" was made by adding the component for "illness": 疒. "That" and "tired" have no connection to "skin" or to each other, but because they shared the same Chinese pronunciation, they shared the same component 皮, which expresses the pronunciation *pi*.

The main component of a kanji, often used to assign it a place in a kanji dictionary, is called a "radical." In the examples here, the kanji for "that" is classified under the radical for "going," and the kanji for "tired" under the radical for "illness." There are countless such examples, making kanji fascinating and complex explorations of symbol and sound. By adding radicals to phonetic components, it was possible to use a limited number of pieces overall to create thousands and thousands of unique, meaningful kanji. You will also discover that a kanji's pronunciation—called its "reading"—is not fixed, but depends on the kanji's meaning and context as well as the language of the speaker, whether he or she is a Chinese person speaking one of many different Chinese dialects, a Korean, or a Japanese.

Onyomi /Kunyomi Readings and Sounds

It is generally thought that *hanzi* came to Japan at the end of the fourth century A.D. as part of Japan's increasing adoption of cultural and religious materials from China, but recent research indicates that *hanzi* may have been introduced into Japan as early as the first or second century A.D. The Japanese adapted Chinese characters (which they would call *kanji*) into their language, using the borrowed ideograms merely to indicate pronunciation, disregarding the original Chinese meanings.

As we mentioned above, kanji can have more than one reading, and in fact most do. What are called *onyomi* readings in Japan are pronunciations that approximate the original Chinese pronunciation and are often used when the kanji is part of a compound, that is, a word made up of more than one kanji character. What are called *kunyomi* readings are native Japanese readings, generally used when a kanji stands alone, either as a complete noun or as an adjective or verb stem. In many cases, the native Japanese word existed before there was a kanji to write it and was simply applied to the corresponding character when it was brought in from China. Similarly, onyomi compounds are often non-native concepts imported from China in civil or religious documents. The difference is a bit like that between Anglo-Saxon words in English, which to our ears seem earthier and more direct, and "imported" Latinate words, which often sound a bit more academic or abstract.

Continuing our example from above, we know that each of the three kanji built on 皮 is pronounced *pi* or *bi* in Chinese. In Japan, the Chinese reading or onyomi of these kanji became *hi*, which was easier for Japanese to pronounce. But each symbol also has its own Japanese pronunciation or kunyomi:

皮 or "skin" is *kawa*
彼 or "that" is *kare*
疲 or "tired" is *tsukare(ru)*

Kanji are used for most verbs, adjectives, and nouns in Japanese. Unlike Chinese, however, the Japanese language can't be written in kanji alone. Also required are two syllable-based writing systems—a cursive *hiragana* and a more angular *katakana* script—each consisting of forty-six phonetic "letters." Hiragana is used to write various grammatical markers, verb and adjective endings, and sometimes adverbs and words whose kanji are no longer in common use. Hiragana are also used to indicate the correct reading and pronunciation of a kanji, especially in books for younger readers. Katakana are used for emphasis and to write foreign, scientific, and onomatopoeic words.

Due to historical divergence, Japanese kanji sometimes have different meanings from the same ideograms currently used in China. Also, in some cases, as with Japanese words like *samurai* and *rōnin* that represent native Japanese concepts and have no Chinese analog, there are no corresponding Chinese readings.

KAISHO

The Kanji Aesthetic

Most Japanese designers like to play with the Western alphabet, just as American and European designers are starting to experiment with kanji. There are many different styles of kanji to work with, each one unique and beautiful.

The original kanji style—a primitive, rounded, natural form first written on bone—is called *kōkotsu moji*. This style developed into a less primitive, more formal style called *kinbun*, which was carved on metal. When written on paper, these shapes evolved into more stylized forms. Many designers today adapt these styles to create an old-fashioned, back-to-nature feeling. A Japanese restaurant in a rustic wooden building specializing in seasonal foods served in handmade earthenware bowls will typeset its menus and signage in one of these more primitive kanji styles, just as organic, natural, and health-food products may use them on their packaging and advertising.

GYOSHO

The first modern kanji style is known as *kaisho* and is a block-print style. As people began to draw calligraphy with brushes, they needed a writing style that flowed more smoothly with the brushstroke, so a cursive style developed. This was called *sōsho*. Although the old style of *sōsho* was created at the end of the second century A.D., a new style of *sōsho* was created in the seventh century to make it easier to write. By the mid-nineteenth century, *sōsho* was the most popular style of writing kanji in Japan.

SŌSHO

When the fountain pen—good for hard, straight lines and not soft brush strokes—was introduced to Japan in the Meiji period (1868–1912) and European-style penmanship became fashionable, the writing style changed back to *kaisho* and has remained that way ever since. The *sōsho* style is now used mainly for calligraphy, but to many Western eyes, it is the form that "looks" most Asian or Japanese, because it is often seen on scrolls in karate and aikido training halls, on movie posters, on menus, and on decorative gift items and other familiar objects.

Many different kanji fonts are used in printed materials. The family of Minchō fonts is used for everyday print, like newspapers and magazines (with its hooklike serifs, Minchō has a bit of the feel of Times Roman, the most common English-language word processor font). The font style known as Gothic (sans serif, a bit like Helvetica) consists of bold, square kanji and is used for advertising and design, as is Pop, a modern, round design that is popular in print and billboard advertising. There are also specialized kanji fonts like Sumō Moji for sumo tournaments and Kantei-ryū for Kabuki theater playbills.

Using This Book

In this book we have included over 130 entries, basing our selections on kanji and kanji compounds we thought were interesting, as well as those commonly found in tattoos and on clothes, accessories, advertisements, greeting cards, and other designs. We've provided a total of five different kanji styles for each entry to represent a different mood or style, from traditional to modern.

The background grid on each page gives you important clues to proportion and position, should you wish to reproduce the kanji by hand. While many people study years to perfect their calligraphy, you can produce reasonably good kanji by following a few basic rules and procedures.

First, make sure each kanji is in the correct position before permanently committing it to paper or skin. Be especially careful that the elements of the kanji aren't reversed from right to left or placed upside down. (We can't count how many times we've seen museum catalogs or books on Japanese culture or Zen with the writing printed upside down!) Be sure to include all the lines (and be sure not to add any new ones!).

Stroke order is crucial. Although not visible to the untrained eye, the order in which the strokes of the kanji are written plays an important role in the overall feeling of the kanji; even a subtle deviation can throw the kanji off-balance. When Japanese is placed vertically on the page, it is read from top to bottom and, if there is more than one line, from right to left. When placed horizontally, it is read from left to right, just like English. The flexibility of kanji to be read either horizontally or vertically makes them aptly suited to being tattooed on various body parts; vertical kanji lines for tubular arms and legs, horizontal kanji lines for broader torsos, backs, and necks.

When writing individual kanji, you also work from left to right. Strokes are written from top to bottom. Horizontal lines are written first, then vertical lines. In general, make the first stroke the top left line. Then draw all the horizontal lines except the bottom line, and then the vertical lines. Finish with the bottom line and add any small accents. The only exception to this stroke order is when you draw box-shaped kanji like 口 or 国. In this case, write the left vertical line first, followed by the top horizontal line and finishing with the right vertical line; then draw the inner kanji and finally add the bottom line. For several books that explain more about writing kanji, see the Bibliography.

For each entry, we give some historical or etymological background, sometimes adding an unusual fact or an anecdote or literary allusion. We have shied away from more fanciful interpretations of the kanji symbols, focusing instead on the actual etymology and background of each kanji for historical accuracy. Pronunciations are provided for all main entries: onyomi readings are in plain type; kunyomi readings are in *italics*. A letter *o* or *u* with a mark above it (ō, ū) indicates that the vowel is slightly extended in length when pronounced, as in the example above of *fūjin* ("Wind God," pronounced *fuujin*) vs. *fujin* ("wife").

Due to our own interests in martial arts, yoga, and Buddhism, we have included many terms from these realms, which are often quite illuminating and rich. There is something for everyone in the Way of Nature, the Way of the Spirit, the Way of the Warrior, and the Way of the Heart, the four broad themes we have used to organized the entries. Zodiac entries that correspond to birth years round out the selection.

Designing with Kanji

Here are just some of the things you can make using kanji in your designs and décor:

- birthday or New Year's cards decorated with the appropriate Zodiac character
- rubber stamps
- seat and cushion covers
- tattoos
- sculptures
- watermarks on stationery
- pastry designs or frosting decorations
- lamp bases
- postcards, greeting cards, and invitations
- handmade jewelry, like brooches and earrings
- curtain and tablecloth motifs
- wall hangings
- carvings and embossings
- glaze finishes on pottery and dishware
- meditation and journal starters
- screensavers on your computer

* * *

People are always fascinated by different cultures, and we continue to be awed by the wonderful ways in which East and West have mingled in culture, lifestyle, design, art, and aesthetics. We hope this book will enrich your own experience of kanji in art and design and help you bring your creative gifts to bear in fresh, new ways.

Just remember: never mistake your "Wife" for the "Wind God"!

We would like to thank Peter Goodman, designer Linda Shimoda, and the staff of Stone Bridge Press for their invaluable help with this project.

Shogo Oketani & Leza Lowitz
TOKYO, JAPAN

The Way of the Warrior

武 者

The Way of the Warrior

The kanji compound *musha* means "samurai warrior." The first kanji 武 (*mu*) means "strength," "bravery," or "weaponry" and combines the two ideograms 戈 (*ka*: "halberd") and 止 (*shi*: "stop"); it literally means "to prevent a soldier's riot with the use of weapons." Modern research indicates that 止 is a simplified rendering of 歩 (*ho*: "walk"), where 武 symbolizes someone walking with a halberd. The second kanji 者 (*sha*) means "person." The title of director Akira Kurosawa's famous movie *Kagemusha* (影武者) means "Shadow Warrior"—a "body double" who pretends to be a samurai lord to prevent the assassination of the real lord, thus foiling the enemy.

武 者　　武 者　　武 者　　武 者

Formal　　　　　Modern　　　　　Flowing　　　　　Stylish

武 (*Bu*) means "strength," "bravery," or "weaponry." Though the radical on the left is the same as *mu* in WARRIOR, here it is pronounced *bu*. 士 (*Shi*) means "a noble-minded person." Originally 士 (*shi*) symbolized a pole stuck into the ground, but it gradually came to mean "work," and by extension "a high-class, well-educated person who works for the good of the nation." Thus, *bushi* means "a stalwart, noble-minded warrior." *Bushi* and the word *samurai* have the same meaning, but to Japanese *bushi* has a more noble, classical connotation. See also FIGHTER.

The Way of the Warrior

Formal   Modern   Flowing   Stylish

武 士 道

武 (*Bu*) means "strength," "bravery,"or "weaponry." 士 (*Shi*) means "a stalwart, noble-minded person." 道 (*Dō*) means "way," "road," or "path." *Bushidō* represents the way of life that a brave and noble-minded person should adhere to, the spiritual path they should travel. The famous seventeenth-century manifesto on samurai ethics, *Hagakure*, states: "The essence of *bushidō* can be found in dying without hesitation." A samurai is someone who can conquer the fear of death and embrace it without showing any attachment to life. See also THE WAY.

武
士
道

武
士
道

武
士
道

武
士
道

Formal

Modern

Flowing

Stylish

The kanji 侍 (*samurai*) was originally read as *saburo*, which meant "to serve the upper class." 侍 is made up of 亻, which symbolizes a person, and 寺, which first meant "public office" but later came to mean "temple." The literal meaning was "a person working for the upper class." In early times, the aristocracy held political power in Japan, and the samurai worked as its army and guardsmen. These highly skilled swordsmen and warriors were called *saburo-mon*, or "serving people." Later, this term evolved to *samurai*. After the tenth century, the samurai started to gain power. By the end of the twelfth century, the first samurai government or *bakufu* was established in Kamakura, south of present-day Tokyo. The samurai class held political as well as military power, and the *shōgun* had far greater power than the emperor. By the mid-nineteenth century, the *shōgun*—a member of the Tokugawa family—was in effect the ruler of Japan, governing from Edo (Tokyo), while the emperor resided hundreds of miles to the south in Kyoto.

侍　　侍　　侍　　侍

The Way of the Warrior

将軍

The ideogram 将 (*shō*) means "leader of soldiers" and 軍 (*gun*) means "army." The original ideogram for 将 was 將. The radical on the left symbolizes a table; the top right element symbolizes meat made as an offering, and the lower right symbolizes a hand. This interesting combination of elements first represented the ritual feast held by an army before battle. Over time, it evolved to mean "to lead." The kanji 軍 symbolizes soldiers surrounding a military cart (車). Samurai originally made up the emperor's military division, and the *shōgun* was the top commander or general of the samurai class, which served the aristocracy.

将軍　　将軍　　将軍　　将軍

　　Formal　　Modern　　Flowing　　Stylish

名 (*Mei*) means "reputation." 誉 (*Yo*) means "to admire." Literally, these ideograms mean "an admired reputation." From the seventeenth to nineteenth centuries, honor was one of the most important samurai virtues. In the highly bureaucratic samurai society of the government, lower-class samurai couldn't rebel against high-class samurai. When a samurai's honor was challenged, he regained it by committing ritual suicide, or *harakiri*, to show he was unafraid of death.

Kanji Facts

The oldest kanji are the inscriptions on animal bones and tortoise carapaces introduced during the days of the twenty-second emperor of the Shang (Yin) dynasty, about 1700–1100 B.C.

The Way of the Warrior

The Way of the Warrior

自 尊 心

自 (*Ji*) means "self." 尊 (*Son*) means "respect." 心 (*Shin*) means "heart/mind." Taken together, these ideograms mean "self-respecting heart." The English word "pride" is usually translated into the Japanese word 誇り (*hokori*), but there is no exact combination of characters for "pride" that uses 誇 because this kind of pride connotes arrogance. In Japan, pride is more a sense of respect and honor that exists quietly inside the individual. Those who possess true pride in the classical Japanese sense do not need to exhibit it to the outside world.

自尊心 自尊心 自尊心 自尊心

Formal   Modern   Flowing   Stylish

The kanji 仁 (*jin*) means "loving and treating others with compassion." 道 (*Dō*) means "the Way" or "path." 仁 is made of two parts: the left side means "human" and the right side means "two." This ideogram thus depicts two people loving and treating each other tenderly and gently. The concept of *jin* is central to Confucian thought, and *jindō* means "the Way of tenderness and compassion." See also COURAGE, GENTLENESS, THE WAY.

The Way of the Warrior

仁道　　仁道　　仁道　　仁道

The Way of the Warrior

The character 義 (*gi*) represents a central concept of Confucian thought. It means "right behavior or action." "Duty" is often translated into Japanese as 義務 (*gimu*), which means "action someone is obligated or bound to take," but 義務 has the nuance of action taken involuntarily. If we take only the first ideogram, 義 (*gi*), the meaning is closer to the English sense of "personal responsibility" or a person's duty to "do the right thing." 義 is made of two radicals: 羊 (*yō*), symbolizing a sheep, which the ancient Chinese saw as a symbol of beauty and passivity and often used as an offering, and 我 (*ga*) meaning "I." The literal meaning of *gi* is "My behavior is in keeping with the right way of action."

Formal　　　　Modern　　　　Flowing　　　　Stylish

正義

The kanji 正 (*sei*) means "to be right" or "correct." 義 (*Gi*) means "right behavior or action." 正 is made of two parts, 一 (*ichi*: "one") and 止 (*shi*: "stop"). Originally this kanji meant "to choose one right thing and stick to it." Interestingly, one of modern Zen master Suzuki Roshi's definitions of enlightenment is "to see one thing through to the end." 正義 thus means "correct way of life."

The Way of the Warrior

正義　　正義　　正義　　正義

義 (*Gi*) means "right behavior or action." 人 (*Jin* or *hito*) means "person." This ideogram represents the side view of a standing figure. 義人 thus suggests "a brave person of moral rectitude who selflessly aids those in need." See also DUTY.

Kanji Facts

According to Chinese historiographer Ts'ang Chieh, kanji were developed over 5,000 years ago when someone saw the footprints of a bird on a snowy field and got the idea to use symbols to express writing.

Formal   Modern   Flowing   Stylish

The Way of the Warrior

This ideogram, when used alone, is pronounced *chikara* and represents the strength and power of a man flexing his biceps. In the kanji compound meaning "sumo wrestler"—力士 (*rikishi*)—力 (*riki*, another reading of this character) is combined with the ideogram 士 (*shi*: "noble-minded person"). See also BUSHI.

力　力　力　力

抵抗

The Way of the Warrior

Both ideograms in this kanji have the same meaning—"defending and rejecting." However, 抵 (*tei*) also means "hitting," and 抗 (*kō*) also means "competing." The left radical in both ideograms is a stylization of 手, meaning "hand." The combination of these ideograms literally means "to defend by hitting with the hands."

抵
抗

抵
抗

抵
抗

抵
抗

Formal

Modern

Flowing

Stylish

叛 逆

叛 (*Han*) means "to disobey and revolt." 逆 (*Gyaku*) means "to be against something." Taken on its own, 叛 can mean "to rebel." John Lennon wore a helmet with the ideogram 叛 on it at the end of the "One to One" concert in Madison Square Garden in 1972. Legend has it that Yoko Ono got the helmet from a Japanese student protestor.

The Way of the Warrior

叛逆　叛逆　叛逆　叛逆

Formal	Modern	Flowing	Stylish

精 気

精 (*Sei*) means "pure and good, the source of all life." 気 (*Ki*), well known in the West by its Chinese pronunciation *chi*, means "life-force energy." 精 is made of 米 ("rice") and 青, which expresses the pronunciation *sei* and symbolizes a translucent blue color like that of clear ocean water; the original meaning of 精 was "polished rice," but it came to mean "pure," "good," or "the source of all life." The ideogram 気 was originally written 氣, a composite of 米 (rice) and 气, which expresses the pronunciation *ki* and means "breath." The original meaning of this older 氣 was "steam from cooked rice." Later, it came to mean "breath," "invisible power," "air," and "feeling." Today the compound 精気 signifies the pure "core power" that all creatures embody and can nurture, the life-force energy that is the underlying power of nature and all sentient beings.

精 精 精 精
気 気 気 気

勇 (*Yū*) means "to be courageous and brave." Here the kanji 気 (*ki*) is used in the sense of "emotion." 勇気 (*Yūki*) thus means "courageous emotion." *Yū* is composed of the ideograms 力 (*chikara*), which means "power and strength," and 甬 (*yō*), which symbolizes the sound of a flower blossoming. See also ENERGY, GENTLENESS, STRENGTH, WISDOM.

Kanji Facts

Some scholars say that kanji were created when the emperor Fu Hsi changed the official method of recording from the "rope knot" method to the "letter" method.

The Way of the Warrior

忠誠

The Way of the Warrior

忠 (*Chū*) means "sincerity" and "devotion." 誠 (*Sei*) means "truthfulness" and "purity of heart." The combination of these ideograms means "to devote oneself with a pure heart." Note that 忠, a central concept of Confucianism, is made of two parts—心 (*kokoro*: "heart") and 中 (*chū*: "middle"). Here, the 中 component expresses the pronunciation *chū* and also means the true feeling deep in the center of the heart. See also HEART.

忠誠　　忠誠　　忠誠　　忠誠

Formal　　　　Modern　　　　Flowing　　　　Stylish

精 力

精 (*Sei*) means "life source." 力 (*Ryoku*, also pronounced *chikara* and *riki*) means "power and strength." The combination of these ideograms symbolizes the source of life's power, which is born from and in turn nurtures sexual energy. See also STRENGTH.

The Way of the Warrior

精
力

精
力

精
力

精
力

復讐

The original meaning of the kanji 復 (*fuku*) was "to return to the original situation," but here it means "retaliation." 讐 (*Shū*) means "enemy." This kanji compound thus means "to retaliate against the enemy." In pre-westernized Japan there was a type of legalized revenge called 仇討ち (*adauchi*); samurai whose lords or fathers had been killed could exact revenge on their enemies to reestablish the strength and solidarity of the clan or family. Many samurai spent their lives looking for revenge. The Edo-period (1603–1867) story of the fabled "Forty-seven Rōnin," in which forty-seven samurai were ordered to commit ritual suicide after successfully killing their former lord's opponent, is one of the most famous examples of samurai seeking to avenge the death of their beloved master.

復讐　復讐　復讐　復讐

浪 (*Rō*) means "wave" and 人 (*nin*) means "person." *Rōnin* were "masterless samurai," professional soldiers who had lost their jobs or been put out of work when their master died. The term came from 浮浪人 (*furōnin*), "floating wave people," that is, the unemployed and homeless. In the Edo period the government decreased the number of lords in order to fatten treasury coffers, and many samurai were prohibited from carrying on their trade. Many *rōnin*, jobless, had to earn their living by repairing paper umbrellas or teaching children. Some of them fell into jobs as bodyguards to *yakuza* gangsters. Others sold their samurai titles to become ordinary civilians. Because many *rōnin*, like the fabled Forty-seven Rōnin, maintained their loyalty long after their master had died, the *rōnin* has been romanticized by modern Japanese as a tragic, faithful hero.

浪人　浪人　浪人　浪人

The Way of the Warrior

Formal　　　　Modern　　　　Flowing　　　　Stylish

無頼

Japanese gangsters, who were originally gamblers and card sharks, take their name from three cards in the playing deck, namely 8 (*ya*), 9 (*ku*), 3 (*san*), which are "useless" as a hand in a card game. These three sounds together became *yakuza*. There are no Chinese ideograms for *yakuza*, so the old name for gambler, 無頼 (*burai*), is used. 無 (*Bu*) is a prefix of negation and 頼 (*rai*) means "to depend or rely on." This compound thus means "outlaw," or "someone living by his own set of rules with no one else to rely on."

無頼　　無頼　　無頼　　無頼

無 敵

無 (*Mu*) means "nothingness," but in this case, the ideogram is used as a prefix of negation, like the English "un-" or "in-." 敵 (*Teki*) means "enemy." The right part of 敵 means "whip," and the left part expresses the pronunciation *teki* and means "object" (or "target"); 敵 thus means "an object hit by a whip." If one can withstand life's blows, one is invincible. This kanji compound means "to be so strong that no enemy in the world exists."

The Way of the Warrior

無
敵

無
敵

無
敵

無
敵

愛 (*Ai*) means "love." 国 (*Koku*) means "country." 心 (*Shin*) means "heart-mind-soul." These ideograms together mean "love one's country with the heart," or "patriotism." Today, most Japanese don't like this term, because the government used it to stir up prowar sentiment during World War II. See also HEART, LOVE.

Formal　　　　　Modern　　　　　Flowing　　　　　Stylish

The radical on the right side of the kanji 剣 means "edge tool." Originally, this ideogram meant "double-edged sword" because these were the kind of swords that first came to Japan from China. Japanese-made swords later evolved into thin curved swords with a single edge. In medieval times, Japanese swords were highly regarded in China for their craft and quality. Historical documents from the end of the fourteenth century show that 9,500 Japanese swords were exported to China around this time. Today Japanese swords are still highly admired for their patterned steel and sophisticated construction that combines strength and sharpness with flexibility, qualities that in past times made them among the most effective weapons for hand combat ever produced.

Kanji Facts

In 1st grade, Japanese kids learn 76 kanji. In 2nd grade, 145. In 3rd grade, 195. In 4th grade, 195. In 5th grade, 195. In 6th grade, 190. After 6th grade, Japanese kids learn 949 "General Use" kanji.

The Way of the Warrior

Formal   Modern   Flowing   Stylish

殺 人 剣

The Way of the Warrior

殺 (*Satsu*) means "kill"; the left part of the kanji expresses the pronunciation *satsu* and the right part symbolizes a spear. 人 (*Jin*) means "person." 剣 (*Ken*) means "sword." Although you might take *satsujinken* to mean a murderous weapon, in fact the term represents the important Zen concept of the sword that cuts through illusion, ego, desire, and authority to reach a state of *mu* (無) or nothingness. A Japanese sword master once said, "We swing the sword not to learn to cut flesh, but to develop the will to adhere to our beliefs." See also SWORD.

殺 人 剣   殺 人 剣   殺 人 剣   殺 人 剣

Formal   Modern   Flowing   Stylish

活 人 劍

Katsujin-ken is an important Zen concept. 活 (*Katsu*) means "to give life." 人 (*Jin*) means "person." And 劍 (*ken*) means "sword." The sword represented here is not a weapon to take life but a sword that gives life to every being in the cosmos. In Zen it is said that both the spirit of *satsujin-ken* and *katsujin-ken* are necessary for cosmic balance. The Zen priest who has this sword in his heart can lead every being to the Pure Land, the Buddhist Paradise. See also SATSUJIN-KEN, SWORD.

活 活 活 活
人 人 人 人
劍 劍 劍 劍

The Way of the Warrior

神 (*Kami*) means "god" or "divine." 風 (*Kaze*) means "wind." *Kamikaze* thus means "divine wind." Although this term is associated with the Japanese Zero fighter pilots' suicide flights in World War II, its history is even older. The term originated as a result of two occasions, in A.D. 1274 and 1281, when Mongolian army ships intent on invading Japanese waters were destroyed by violent storms. On both occasions, the Japanese samurai army had been completely defeated by the Mongolian army. But at night, on each occasion, storms came seemingly out of nowhere and sank almost the entire Mongolian fleet. Since then, Japanese came to believe the *kamikaze* would blow whenever their country was in danger. During World War II, many lives were lost to this futile Japanese military strategy. See also WIND GOD.

神風   神風   神風   神風

Formal   Modern   Flowing   Stylish

忍者

忍 (*Nin*) originally meant "to endure in the face of danger." 者 (*Ja*) means "person." 忍 is made of two parts; the upper part 刃 expresses the pronunciation *nin* and means "blade," and beneath is 心, or "heart" (thus the idea of surviving "even with a blade poised above the heart"). The native Japanese reading of 忍 is *shinobi*, and in this case the kanji has evolved to mean "to keep a secret" or "to hide oneself." In the twelfth century, ninja warriors were mountain people who worked as skilled spies for samurai. By the sixteenth century, they had become invaluable assassins, informants, and espionage agents employed by the warring feudal lords. Men, women, and even dogs were used as ninja warriors. See also HEART.

The Way of the Warrior

忍者   忍者   忍者   忍者

The Way of the Warrior

戦 (*Sen*) means "fight" and 士 (*shi*) means "noble-man." This combination of ideograms can refer to any warrior, not just someone from the "elite" samurai class. Moreover, it suggests a warrior with a noble soul. The ideogram 戦 is made of two parts, 戈 (*ka*: "halberd") and 単, which expresses the sound of the ancient Chinese pronunciation *zen*, which is similar to *sen*. See also BUSHI.

Kanji Facts

Chinese books were first brought to Japan via Korea between the third and fifth centuries A.D. The Japanese then borrowed the Chinese writing system in its entirety by adopting classical Chinese as the official written language.

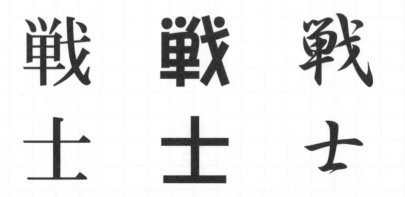

Musashi

武蔵

Musashi is the name of great seventeenth-century Japanese sword master Miyamoto Musashi, who wrote the seminal work on warrior strategy, *The Book of Five Rings*. Born of humble origins and named Takezō, he decided to change his name when he became a samurai. At that time, the area currently known as Tokyo was called Musashi—using the ideograms 武蔵—so he took that as his name. 武 (*Mu*) means "strength," and its kunyomi pronunciation is *takeru* (which was close to his given name); the onyomi of 蔵 is *zō*.

武蔵   武蔵   武蔵   武蔵

羅 生 門

The Way of the Warrior

This kanji compound became famous from Akira Kurosawa's movie (starring Toshiro Mifune) of the same title. It is the name of a gateway to Kyoto built at the end of the eighth century. The original name of this elaborate arch was 羅城門 (*rajōmon*), which means "outer castle gate." In the eleventh century, with the fall of the aristocracy, the gateway went to ruin. It was believed that demons lived there. The current form of the name came into use in the seventeenth century and now, thanks to the popularity of the film, suggests a world in which there are no absolute truths, only shifting perspectives.

羅生門　羅生門　羅生門　羅生門

| Formal | Modern | Flowing | Stylish |

座頭市

The fictional blind swordsman Zatōichi traveled throughout Japan in the early 1800s, making his living as a gambler and masseuse. In medieval times, 座頭 (*zatō*) denoted the low rank of a blind lute player. Later, it was used for blind people in general. Thus: "Blind Ichi." A popular film series starring Katsu Shintarō focused on this lone-wolf *yakuza*, who despite his disability could "sense" the movements of his enemies and in an instant cut them down, usually in the cause of righting a wrong. (A new *Zatōichi* series has been released starring popular *yakuza* film actor and director "Beat" Takeshi Kitano.)

The Way of the Warrior

座頭市   座頭市   座頭市   座頭市

風 林 火 山

The Way of the Warrior

"Fūrinkazan" is the famous motto of the army led by Takeda Shingen, a powerful sixteenth-century samurai warlord. (Akira Kurosawa's film *Kagemusha* is about the man who became his double or decoy.) The term originally came from the ancient Chinese military strategist Sun-Tzu's book *The Art of War* (so popular today with corporate executives and powerbrokers). 風 (*Fū*) means "wind," 林 (*rin*) means "forest, 火 (*ka*) means "fire," and 山 (*zan*) means "mountain." The phrase thus means "move swiftly like the wind (風), stay quiet like the forest (林), attack fiercely like fire (火), and be steady like the mountain (山)."

風
林
火
山

風
林
火
山

風
林
火
山

風
林
火
山

Formal   Modern   Flowing   Stylish

風 神

風 (*Fū*) means "wind" and 神 (*jin*) means "god." 神 is made of
ネ, which symbolizes divine service, and 申, which originally meant
"thunderbolt." In ancient China, it was believed that the gods con-
trolled everything, even the mysterious workings of nature. The Wind
God in Japan is derived from a Hindu deity integrated into Buddhism
and is drawn as a muscular figure called a demon, or *oni*, holding a
big bag full of the wind he gathers from the sky. Note that the two
kanji here are the same as in *kamikaze* ("divine wind"), except their
order is reversed. In *kamikaze*, the kanji use their kunyomi or native
Japanese pronunciations, while in *fūjin* the pronunciations are both
onyomi. See also DEMON, KAMIKAZE.

The Way of the Warrior

風 神   風 神   風 神   風 神

Formal	Modern	Flowing	Stylish	

雷 神

雷 (*Rai*) means "thunder" and 神 (*Jin*) means "god. The Thunder God derives from a Hindu deity integrated into Buddhism. In Japan this god has been drawn as a muscular demon or *oni* figure like the Wind God, but he has drums on his back and holds sticks in both hands. In Japan, parents warn their children, "If you sleep with your belly button showing, the Thunder God will steal it." See also RAIN, WIND GOD.

雷 神   雷 神   雷 神   雷 神

Formal   Modern   Flowing   Stylish

不動明王

The Japanese name for one of the Buddhas in Tantric Buddhism, Fudōmyōō is a translation of Acalan, which is Sanskrit for the 745th name of Lord Vishnu and means "the unmovable, unwavering one" who is "unshakable from his own nature, power, and knowledge." 不動 (*Fudō*) combines two kanji for "no movement" and means "esteemed," and 明王 (*myōō*), representing "bright king," means "lord." This Buddha sits scowling fiercely in the middle of a fire, holding a sword. *Yakuza* (gangsters) often get tattoos of images of Fudōmyōō because they want to look strong.

不動明王 不動明王 不動明王 不動明王

The Way of the Warrior

Formal　　　Modern　　　Flowing　　　Stylish　　47

覚 悟

The Way of the Warrior

Both 覚 (*kaku*) and 悟 (*go*) have the same meaning—"to become aware," "to awaken," or "to attain spiritual enlightenment." Originally this kanji compound meant "to learn the truth by shedding evil desires." But it now means "having the strong determination to take action at the risk of one's own life."

Kanji Facts

In A.D. 712, the imperial anthology known as the *Kojiki* (Record of Ancient Matters) used Chinese characters to write Japanese words and endings, mainly by using characters for their phonetic values.

覚
悟

覚
悟

覚
悟

覚
悟

Formal   Modern   Flowing   Stylish

鉄 拳

鉄 (*Tetsu*) means iron. The radical 金 on the left side of *tetsu* (鉄) symbolizes "metal." 拳 (*Ken*) means "fist"; the lower part of the second kanji 拳 is 手, which symbolizes a hand with five fingers, and the upper part means "top" (the top of the hand is the "fist"). The Japanese pronunciation of 拳 (*ken*) evolved from the original Chinese pronunciation *quan* in Shaolin-Quan (少林拳), a martial practice that is considered the origin of all Asian combat arts. For obvious reasons, Japanese boxers like to use this term—"Iron Fist"—as a ring name.

The Way of the Warrior

鉄拳 鉄拳 鉄拳 鉄拳

用 心 棒

The Way of the Warrior

用心 (*Yōjin*) means "to prepare for an emergency." 用 (*Yō*) means "to use." 心 (*Shin* or *jin*) means "the heart," which here represents "mindfulness." The original meaning of 棒 (*bō*) is "wooden stick." This kanji compound thus means "to be mindful or mentally prepared in case of emergency." *Yōjinbō* originally referred to an actual wooden stick used in emergencies, but the meaning has evolved to mean "bodyguard." These days, a *yōjinbō* is generally a person who works as a guard at a casino, bar, or disco, or as a *yakuza* sideman. It's also the title of one of Akira Kurosawa's famous movies starring Toshiro Mifune as a loyal bodyguard. See also HEART.

用
心
棒

用
心
棒

用
心
棒

用
心
棒

Formal   Modern   Flowing   Stylish

The Way of the Heart

The Way of the Heart

This ideogram is said to represent the shape of the human heart; the short lines on either side of the center line symbolize the chambers and aorta. *Kokoro* can mean "middle," as in "the heart of things," but like its English counterpart, the word "heart" has so many nuances and deeper meanings—"spirit," "emotion," "will," "affection," and "kindness"—that it's often considered untranslatable. Among its diverse usages, *kokoro* symbolizes the emotional appreciation of beauty, as in this *tanka* by Saigyō, the famous medieval Japanese poet, who wrote, *Kokoro naki minimo awareha shirarekeri, shigi tatsu sawano akino yugure:*

> Even my poor heart / unable to appreciate beauty— / is touched by the snipes / flying out of the autumn sunset / at the marsh.

Formal   Modern   Flowing   Stylish

This character shows the element 口, which means "mouth," next to the element 禾, which expresses the old pronunciation of this ideogram, *kwa. Kwa* has the same meaning as 会 (*kai*) , which means "to meet." Namely, "mouths (people) meet and harmonize." *Wa* is one of the most highly valued concepts in Japan, and it has long been central to the Japanese lifestyle of "harmony and consensus." The original meaning of this ideogram is "to respond," but it has other meanings, such as "to become soft," "quiet," "calm," or "joined." Shōtoku Taishi, the revered seventh-century Japanese statesman, considered harmony central to living a peaceful life, and in his famous Constitution of Seventeen Articles he stated, "和 (*Wa*) is what we should most respect."

Formal　　　　Modern　　　　Flowing　　　　Stylish

The Way of the Heart

The ideogram 平 (*hei*) means "flat" and is composed of a combination of stylized forms of 于, which means "balanced energy," and 八 , which means "energy that doesn't stagnate." 和 (*Wa*) means "harmony." *Heiwa* thus suggests that when opposing forces meet, they balance each other to create calmness and smooth movement. In modern Japan, each emperor's reign is given a name; the current imperial era is called 平成 (Heisei), using the same character 平 to denote the nation's hopes for a peaceful and smooth development. See also HARMONY.

平和 平和 平和 平和

Formal   Modern   Flowing   Stylish

Humility is highly valued in Japan. 謙 (*Ken*) means "modesty" and "to yield" and is made of two parts. The left part 言 means "say" and the right part 兼 expresses the pronunciation *ken*. The kanji also means "restraint" and originally meant "to restrain oneself from talking too much." 遜 (*Son*) means "to humble oneself"; the right side is "grandchild" or 孫 (*son*), which also means "to resign one's position," perhaps meaning passing it down to one's grandchild. The right and left sides together mean "to let other people go ahead." The quality of *kenson* is embodied in the Japanese penchant for modestly deflecting praise. When Japanese give presents to their friends, they often say, "This is a very useless, cheap thing, but please accept it anyway," even if the gift is quite expensive or desirable.

The Way of the Heart

謙遜　謙遜　謙遜　謙遜

| Formal | Modern | Flowing | Stylish |

The Way of the Heart

This ideogram for "self" depicts three horizontal strings joined by two vertical strings, representing the understanding that we are all joined, yet must know ourselves first before we can know others. The fourteenth-century essayist Kenkō Yoshida wrote in *Tsurezuregusa* ("Essays in Idleness"), "Someone who knows himself can be called someone who knows everything." See also INDEPENDENCE.

Kanji Facts

In the Heian period (A.D. 794–1185), men of letters and government studied the new language written in kanji. Women spent their time perfecting their skills in their native language and as a result produced great works of literature like *The Tale of Genji*.

Formal   Modern   Flowing   Stylish

This ideogram has two parts. The upper part 羊 (*hitsuji*) means "sheep" and shows the animal's face and horns, and the lower part 大 (*dai*) means "big" and shows a figure with outstretched arms and legs. Sheep were revered as peace-loving and gentle creatures and were used in sacred offerings. Over time, the meaning of this kanji evolved into a general notion of goodness, docility, and beauty. Those who exist in harmony with nature, keeping their innocence, are considered beautiful, mature beings.

The Way of the Heart

Formal   Modern   Flowing   Stylish

The Way of the Heart

The original meaning of this ideogram was "to be right" or "to play music and song in the right key." The meaning later evolved to connote "grace" and "elegance." The left side 牙 expresses the onyomi pronunciation *ga*, and the right side 隹 means "small bird." The kanji may thus symbolize the elegant shape of a small bird. In Japan, 雅 is not generally used to express the notion of being touched by the divine, as the term "grace" or its equivalent might suggest in other languages and cultures. Rather, it is often used to express the ancient culture of Kyoto and the many artistic traditions from Japan's imperial court—located there some thirteen hundred years ago—that are still evident in the tastes and styles of the modern city.

雅   雅   雅   雅

Formal   Modern   Flowing   Stylish

This ideogram means "truth" but also "sincerity" or "truthful heart." The left side 言 means "say." The right side 成 expresses the onyomi pronunciation *sei* and means "result." This kanji originally meant "to state the truth about one's own actions." *Chūyō*, an ancient Chinese book on Confucianism, states: "誠 (Truth) is the main way of the universe, and having 誠 is the Way of humanity." In *Taboo*, Nagisa Oshima's film, the nineteenth-century samurai faction Shinsengumi that was defending the Tokugawa government used this ideogram as its fighting symbol.

誠　誠　誠　誠

The Way of the Heart

The Way of the Heart

The upper part of the ideogram means "knowledge" and is made of two elements—矢 (*ya*) or "arrow" on the left and 口 (*kuchi*) or "mouth" on the right. To have knowledge is to speak one's mind as fast and sharp as an arrow. The lower ideogram is 日 (*hi*: "sun"), symbolizing illumination. 智 (*Chi*) is an important concept in Confucianism; *Chūyō*, an ancient Chinese Confucian text, places it among the three most important concepts of humanity: 智 (*chi*: "wisdom"), 仁 (*jin*: "gentleness"), and 勇 (*yū*: "bravery"). See also COURAGE, GENTLENESS.

智   智   智   智

寛容

寛 (*Kan*) means "wide," "big," or "soft." 容 (*Yō*) means "to put food into a bowl." Together, these ideograms mean "a big mind that can hold many things." The upper part of 寛 symbolizes a roof. Its original meaning was "a big house that has enough space to accommodate many people." Though we normally think of generosity as meaning "giving," it is interesting to note how the quality of "receptivity" is inherent in this word, which literally illustrates how generosity means to be spacious and open to receive.

The Way of the Heart

寛容　寬容　寛容　寬容

Formal	Modern	Flowing	Stylish

The Way of the Heart

Morality is a central concept of Confucianism. The ideogram 礼 is a modernization of 禮, which is made of two parts: 示 on the left signifies the divine, and 豊 means "offering." The literal meaning is "to make an offering to the gods." It originally meant the proper way to make an offering, but it evolved to mean "everyday morality," or "the rules for right living." A disciple of Confucius asked, "What do you think of the man who isn't servile even in poverty, and the man who isn't arrogant even in prosperity?" Confucius answered, "He's a good man, but he's not as great as the man who knows how to enjoy a moral life even in poverty, and the man who is good-mannered to everyone, even though he's rich."

礼　　　礼　　　礼　　　礼

Formal　　　Modern　　　Flowing　　　Stylish

清

This ideogram originally represented a stream of clear water. The left part (the three "droplets") symbolizes water, and the right side represents the pronunciation _sei_. The kanji also means "blue," like the color of clear water. Kiyomizu-dera (清水寺), the famous temple on stilts in eastern Kyoto, uses this kanji in its name, a reference to the clear spring water flowing down from the mountain nearby.

Kanji Facts

Kanji represent ideas or words rather than letters or syllables. They have different meanings and pronunciations depending on how they are combined with other kanji.

The Way of the Heart

清　　　清　　　清　　　清

Formal　　　　Modern　　　　Flowing　　　　Stylish

The Way of the Heart

This kanji consists of elements that mean "coldness surrounded by ice." It is used to express a sense of bracing clarity or rejuvenation, a sense of exhilaration such as comes from soaking in an outdoor hot spring in the snow and then standing up and feeling the cold mountain air against your skin.

Formal   Modern   Flowing   Stylish

献身

献 (*Ken*) means "to consecrate" or "to make an offering." 身 (*Shin*) means "human body" (originally "pregnant woman"). The original ideogram of 献 is 獻, whose left part is a bowl with a tiger design; the right part 犬 means "dog" and expresses the pronunciation *ken* but suggests dog meat, often used as an offering. The term *kenshin* thus literally means "to make an offering of the body." In the eighth century, the emperor invited the Chinese Buddhist priest Ganjin to Japan to ordain Buddhist priests, but each time Ganjin attempted to go he encountered an obstacle that made the trip impossible. At sixty-five, after four failed attempts, Ganjin finally reached Japan's shores. But conditions on the ship were bad, and food was scarce, so Ganjin went blind. The Japanese were deeply impressed by Ganjin's devotion to Buddhism, for which he literally gave up parts of his body.

The Way of the Heart

献身　献身　献身　献身

情

This ideogram means "emotion" but also means "mercy" and "love." The radical on the left is a variant form of 心 ("heart"), while the element 青 on the right expresses the Chinese pronunciation *sei* or *jō*. The opposite of 情 (*jō*) is 理 (*ri*), meaning "logic." Japanese culture has long prized tragedies in which human emotion overrides logic. One of the most famous plays of the Bunraku puppet theater is the seventeenth-century drama *Love Suicide at Sonezaki* by Chikamatsu Monzaemon. The play tells the story of a doomed love affair between a merchant and a courtesan forced to commit double suicide to prove their love. 情死 (*Jōshi*), the word for this kind of tragic "love suicide," combines the kanji for "love/emotion" with 死 (*shi:* "death"). See also PASSION.

情　情　情　情

情熱

The literal translation of this kanji is "hot emotion" or "emotional fever," since 情 (*jō*) means "emotion" and 熱 (*netsu*) means "fever" or "hot/heated." The upper part of 熱 symbolizes a burst of energy, and the four points below symbolize fire. As a whole, Japanese people are more known for their calm restraint than their hot-headed passion. Kabuki drama, however, provides many passionate characters. One of the most famous is O-Shichi, a sixteen-year-old girl who fell in love with a young priest at a temple where her family had taken refuge from a fire. After the family returned home, she couldn't get him out of her mind and finally set her house afire so that she could return to the temple. The fire was quickly put out, but O-Shichi was sentenced to death. In old Japan, where a single house on fire could destroy a whole town of paper-and-wood houses, arson was a serious crime.

The Way of the Heart

情
熱

情
熱

情
熱

情
熱

憐 憫

The Way of the Heart

Both kanji in this compound—憐 (*ren*) and 憫 (*bin*)—mean "to be compassionate," "to be sympathetic," and "to take pity." Both kanji also have another kunyomi pronunciation: *awaremi*. The left part of 憐 symbolizes the heart; the right part expresses the pronunciation *ren* and symbolizes a fluid situation. It originally meant "to pay continuous attention." The left part of 憫 also symbolizes the heart; the right side expresses the pronunciation *bin* and means "to worry" and "to sympathize." In the seventeenth century, the fifth *shōgun* Tokugawa Tsunayoshi decreed an Order of Compassion to Animals. The *shōgun* had been born in the Year of the Dog, and his decree stated that people should treat dogs with special kindness. Though his intentions were good, before long there were many stray dogs wandering the streets. See also LOVE.

憐 憐 憐 憐
憫 憫 憫 憫

The left side of this ideogram symbolizes the divine, and the right side expresses the Japanese pronunciation *fuku*. Pleasing the gods leads to happiness, both divine and human. At Shinto shrine harvest festivals you often see sacred Kagura dancers wearing the comical white mask of the rosy-cheeked woman Otafuku (お多福), whose name means "great happiness" and whose movements are intended to give the gods pleasure.

The Way of the Heart

福　福　福　福

The Way of the Heart

This ideogram originally meant "spacious" but has evolved to mean "kind," "excellent," "good," "generous," and "able." Osamu Dazai, the popular "decadent" novelist who committed suicide in 1948, commented that this ideogram 優, made of two parts—亻 symbolizing a person, and 憂 meaning "to feel sad and grieve"—in essence shows how a person who can feel sadness has a kind heart. See also COMPASSION.

Kanji Facts

The characters used in Japan are basically the same as those used in China. Japanese kanji derive from the same tradition as classical Chinese, but Japanese uses fewer characters, and there are many post-classical Chinese words that are not normally used in Japanese.

Formal   Modern   Flowing   Stylish

歓 喜

The first kanji of this compound, 歓 (*kan*), means "to enjoy"; the left component expresses the pronunciation and the right part 欠 symbolizes an open mouth. The second kanji 喜 (*ki*) can mean "to enjoy" and is made of two parts—the top is the left side of the kanji 鼓 ("drum") and the bottom is the kanji 口 for "mouth." *Kanki* is a Buddhist term (also pronounced *kangi*) that means "to feel joy through understanding the teachings of Buddha," suggesting perhaps ritual chanting and the beating of a drum.

The Way of the Heart

歓 喜   歓 喜   歓 喜   歓 喜

The Way of the Heart

希 (*Ki*) means "to desire" and 望 (*bō*) means "to look forward to."
The top part メ of 希 symbolizes a crossed thread, and the lower part
布 means "cloth." Its original meaning was "a small stitched cloth,"
and this later evolved to mean "rare " and "want." Instead of 亡 the
original ideogram of 望 used the element 臣, which means "eye"; 月
on the upper right means "moon." The lower part represents a person
standing up. Thus the character suggests looking into the distance or
"to wish for something," waiting patiently for it to happen and looking forward to its fulfillment. Desire is inextricably linked to antici-
pation. Here is the boyhood wish of Chūya Nakahara, the Taishō-era
poet and lyricist: "*I wish the earth would break in half, and one half
would travel abroad. Then, I would just sit on the remaining half
and look up at the blue sky.*" What is *your* wish?

Formal	**Modern**	**Flowing**	**Stylish**

The kanji 安 (*an*) means "safe," "calm," and "settled." The upper part of this ideogram symbolizes a roof, and the lower part is the kanji 女 (*onna:* "woman"). Originally, the character symbolized a woman priest at a Chinese shrine; her presence was thought to insure that the worship service would be a success. The kanji on the right, 全 (*zen*), means "to be complete," "whole," or "total." The bottom part 王 means "jewel," and in ancient China the character meant "a flawless jewel." See also TRANQUILLITY.

The Way of the Heart

| Formal | Modern | Flowing | Stylish |

衆道

The Way of the Heart

The kanji compound 衆道 is the old Japanese term for "homosexual."
(There is no separate term for "lesbian.") Originally, homosexuality
was called 若衆道 (*wakashūdō*), which means, roughly "[following]
the Way (道) of young boys (若 衆)." Before westernization in the
nineteenth century, homosexuality was not taboo in Japan but, as in
ancient Greece, was embraced by the upper classes, particularly the
samurai warriors. Bisexuality was in fact the norm for Japanese men
from samurai to ordinary citizens. In the fourteenth century, Ashi-
kaga Takauji, the first *shōgun* of the Muromachi government, formed
a horseback battalion of his young male lovers, called the Hanaikki
(花一揆), or "Flower Corps."

衆道　衆道　衆道　衆道

　Formal　　**Modern**　　**Flowing**　　**Stylish**

The Way of the Heart

This kanji is made of a combination of the elements 欠 ("mouth") and 哥 ("to sing a song"; note the two "mouths" 口). The left radical also expresses the onyomi pronunciation of *ka*. In Japanese, the term 歌 (*uta*) is synonymous with 短歌 (*tanka*), the ancient Japanese court poems from the Heian period (A.D. 794–1185) that were sung aloud and consisted of thirty-one syllables in distinct units of 5-7-5-7-7. The first three units eventually became the shorter seventeen-syllable form of poetry known as haiku. Many *uta* were composed as love poems in the Heian period. See also POEM.

The Way of the Heart

This kanji is composed of the element 言 ("word") combined with 寺 ("temple"). 寺 originally meant "public office," and 詩 meant "sentences written correctly." In ancient Japan, *shi* meant "poem in the Chinese style" as distinct from the formal Japanese verse 短歌 (*tanka*). In ancient times, the Japanese used the term 詩歌 (*shika*) to mean "poem," but now 詩 (*shi*) refers to a free-verse poem in the European style. See also SONG, SPIRIT OF THE WORD.

詩　詩　詩　詩

独 (*Doku*) means "to be alone," and 立 (*ritsu*) means "to stand up." The literal meaning of this kanji is thus "to stand up by oneself" or "to stand on one's own." The original ideogram of 独 was 獨, but as this was too complex to write, the form was simplified. The radical on the left means "animal," and the character originally illustrated a pack of dogs biting each other. Later, the meaning evolved into its opposite; rather than "pack," it now means "alone."

The Way of the Heart

独
立

独
立

独
立

独
立

探 求

The Way of the Heart

The first kanji 探 (*tan*) means "to search deeply."
求 (*Kyū*) means "to seek." A quest is a journey, a
profound spiritual search seeking out one's path.
The left part of 探 symbolizes a hand, so this character contains the meaning "searching by hand." 求
illustrates "fur sticking out." One has to dig deep
beneath the skin to find direction.

Kanji Facts

Japan created its own
characters when it could not
find appropriate Chinese
ideograms to represent a
Japanese word. These are
known as *kokuji*, or "national
characters."

探 求   探 求   探 求   探 求

Formal   **Modern**   **Flowing**   **Stylish**

安 (*An*) means "safe," "calm," and "settled." 泰 (*Tai*) means "big" or "mellow." To be tranquil is to be calm and completely mellow. Lao-tzu, the ancient Chinese philosopher, said a tranquil life is one in which "people enjoy even cheap food, are comfortable in cheap clothes, and are content to live in small houses." Tranquillity and calm may exist in the house of small desires. 泰 symbolizes both hands being put into a river to scoop up water. Water flowing smoothly is tranquillity. See also SAFETY.

The Way of the Heart

安泰
安泰
安泰
安泰

契り

り

契り (*chigiri*) is the old Japanese term for sexual intercourse. It originally meant "promise from a past life" but later evolved to mean "promise to be husband and wife" and "sex." The kanji 契 is made of two parts, the upper meaning "sword" and the lower "person." It originally represented carving a person's head as a means of branding and claiming ownership. Later, it came to mean simply "contract," or "promise." These days, the term *chigiri* means "marriage vow" but is also considered a very elegant literary term for "sex." It applies to relations between the opposite and same sexes, and it appears often in the eleventh-century Japanese novel *The Tale of Genji* to describe the shining prince's exploits. Use of this word carries the nuance that a couple who had a past life connection have reunited in this lifetime with the promise of love and sexual bliss.

契
り

契
り

契
り

契
り

沈 黙

The first kanji 沈 (*chin*) means "to sink" or "to go down in the water." 黙 (*Moku*) means "to be silent." Literally, this kanji compound means "to sink into silence." The novelist Shūsaku Endō intended the word in its fullest sense when he chose it as the title for his novel about the prohibition of Christianity in seventeenth-century Japan. When the Spanish priest Rodriguez was arrested by the *shōgun*'s government for preaching Christianity, he asked Jesus why He couldn't save those who were being tortured and made to suffer for the sake of the Lord. But Jesus answered in silence. Rodriguez, forced to trample on Jesus's image, become an apostate to save the Japanese believers. When he stepped on the image, once again Jesus offered acceptance in silence.

The Way of the Heart

沈 黙   沈 黙   沈 黙   沈 黙

Formal	Modern	Flowing	Stylish	

想像

The Way of the Heart

The first kanji 想 (*sō*) means "to think" or "to imagine." 像 (Zō) means "object" or "shape." This kanji literally means "to imagine a shape," but the original meaning of this term was "to imagine an elephant" (the radical on the right—象—means "elephant" and is pronounced *zō*). Elephants lived in southern China around 1500 B.C. when the kanji 象 was first created, but by 1000 B.C. these animals had completely perished and no one alive then had ever actually seen one. So when these later Chinese saw elephant bones brought in from Southeast Asia they could only imagine the shape of this enormous animal. That is how the kanji compound 想像 meaning "imagination" came to be made of the ideograms for "imagine" (想) and "the shape of an elephant" (象).

想像　　　想像　　　想像　　　想像

Formal　　　　Modern　　　　Flowing　　　　Stylish

The Way
of Nature

自然

The Way of Nature

陰陽

Nature and human nature dance between light and dark, sun and moon, male and female, day and night. The balance and embrace of opposite forces is at the heart of the Chinese view of the cosmos. The kanji for *in* (陰) represents a hill covered by a shelter or roof (今), symbolizing shade, coolness, and a negative charge. The kanji for *yō* (陽) represents a sunny, open space, symbolizing light, warmth, and a positive charge. Emptiness cannot exist without fullness, nor light without dark. *In* is considered feminine energy, and *yō* is considered masculine. The familiar symbol ☯ of complementary shapes and shades represents this concept of eternal balance.

陰　　陰　　陰　　陰
陽　　陽　　陽　　陽

大 地

The kanji 大 (*dai*) represents a person with arms and legs spread in an open posture of receptivity and means "big" or "great." *Chi* (地) means "land"; the radical 土 on the left indicates "soil," and the right part 也 is said to have originally symbolized a vagina. The great Earth Mother is revered in Japanese culture. The common Japanese translation of "Planet Earth" is *chikyū* (地球), but 大地 (*daichi*) is a less-scientific and more poetic-sounding term.

The Way of Nature

大地　　大地　　大地　　大地

The first kanji 大 (*tai*) means "big" or "great." 気 (*Ki*) represents the life-force energy within us (also called *qi* or *chi* in Chinese and *prana* in Sanskrit), but it also means "invisible power," "the meeting of earth and sky," and "breath." Here, 気 is used to mean "air"—the air that covers the entire earth; the form is a simplification of the original Chinese character 氣, which symbolized the steam rising from cooked rice. The common Japanese translation of "air" is *kūki* (空気), a more scientific term. See also ENERGY.

大気 大気 大気 大気

This character symbolizes water flowing smoothly. To cultivate equanimity, we should allow the challenges of life to flow around us, like a river around rock. Lao-tzu said, "The highest good is like water. Water gives benefit to all beings in this world. It never fights. Furthermore, it is content to stay in a humble place."

Kanji Facts

After WWII, Japan simplified many kanji. In 1950, China did the same, but more radically. Hong Kong and Taiwan still use many traditional, unsimplified Chinese characters.

The Way of Nature

水   水   水   水

Formal   Modern   Flowing   Stylish

The Way of Nature

This kanji represents a burning flame. Fire has long been revered by many ancient world cultures as a symbol of purification and renewal. Throughout Japan, fire ceremonies are sacred rituals held in shrines and temples to this day. One of the most famous is the Mt. Kurama Fire Festival, or Kurama no Hi Matsuri (鞍馬の火祭り), which is held annually in northern Kyoto on the night of October 22 and features people running through the mountains carrying hundreds of brightly lit torches to welcome the gods.

Formal   Modern   Flowing   Stylish

This kanji is in the shape of three peaks, symbolizing a mountain spreading the energy contained within it outward. Some 75 percent of Japan's land mass is mountainous, and since ancient times mountains in Japan were considered sacred bridges from this world to the spirit world. Legend has it that the massive mountain gods loved to practice sumo wrestling with each other.

The Way of Nature

Formal	Modern	Flowing	Stylish

This ideogram symbolizes a stream or a river. Water flows swiftly down mountain streams, evoking the Buddhist concept of *mujō*, (無常) or "transience," that is, a state of constant change where nothing remains as it is from one moment to the next. Japan has its own version of Heraclitus' famous dictum "You can't step in the same river twice." The twelfth-century poet Kamo-no-Chōmei wrote, "The flowing river never stops and yet the water never stays the same."

Kanji Facts

How many kanji are there? The Japan Industrial Standard (JIS) says there are about 6,000.

Formal   Modern   Flowing   Stylish

The three droplets on the left side of this character symbolize water, and the element on the right symbolizes grass growing abundantly. The kanji thus represents a great and powerful flow of water, like the vast ocean. The original ideogram for "ocean" contained the character 母 (*haha*: "mother") in the lower right. In French, the ocean is *la mer*, and mother is *la mère*. Tatsuji Miyoshi, a modernist poet, wrote of this strange connection that cuts across languages and cultures:

> Ocean, in the language we use / there is a mother inside you / And mother, in the language the French use / there is an ocean inside you.

The Way of Nature

The Way of Nature

This kanji symbolizes a crescent shape. In Japanese, the full moon is called *jūgoya* (十五夜), which means "fifteenth night." The most beautiful moon of the year is said to be the full moon in September. On that night, people hold a moon-viewing ceremony called *tsukimi* (月見) and offer dumplings (and verse) to express gratitude to our celestial companion.

月　　月　　月　　月

Formal　　　　Modern　　　　Flowing　　　　Stylish

日 輪

This kanji compound means "a round and shining sun." 日 (*Nichi*) symbolizes a shining sun and also means "day." *Rin* (輪) means "circle." The element 車 on the left of 輪 means "vehicle," and the element 侖 on the right represents a round shape and expresses the pronunciation *rin*. The customary Japanese word for "sun" is *taiyō* (太陽), but *nichirin* has a more classical, poetic sound.

The Way of Nature

日 輪   日 輪   日 輪   日 輪

The Way of Nature

This kanji meaning "flower" is a combination of the symbols for "grass" (top) and "change" (bottom). The "change" element 化 also expresses the onyomi pronunciation *ka*. The fleeting beauty of the cherry blossom, which shines brightly for but a very short time before its petals fall or are swept away by the wind, embodies the idea of change and has come to symbolize Japanese aesthetic taste. The most beautiful cherry blossoms are on Mt. Yoshino in Nara Prefecture. Saigyō, the Japanese poet who lived in seclusion on Mt. Yoshino, wrote, "I wish I could die under the full cherry blossoms / on the full moon of February / when Buddha entered Nirvana." Saigyō in fact got his wish and died on February 16, 1190. See also NIRVANA.

花 花 花 花

Formal   Modern   Flowing   Stylish

The Way of Nature

This kanji contains 虫 (*mushi*), the ideogram for "insect," because the ancient Chinese believed it was the blowing wind that gave birth to insects. The Japanese consider wind one of the most beautiful of the four primary elements of nature—along with flowers, birds, and the moon—collectively referred to as *kachōfūgetsu* (花鳥風月). Bashō wrote often of the wind, as in this haiku:

Mt. Arashi— / inside the growing bush / a stream of wind

See also KAMIKAZE, WIND GOD.

The Way of Nature

This kanji is made of three parts—天 ("heaven"), 冂 ("cloud"), and 水 ("water")—and looks like raindrops falling against a pane of glass. In Japan, there are two rainy seasons—in June and October. The June summer rainy season is called *baiu* (梅雨), which means "plum rain" (plum trees bear fruit around this time). The October rainy season is called *akisame* (秋雨), which means "autumn rain" (*aki* means "autumn" and *same* is the old pronunciation of *ame*). The rains of *baiu* are especially important because they help the rice that was planted in May grow strong. See also WATER.

Formal   Modern   Flowing   Stylish

The upper part of this character, a stylized form of 火, symbolizes "fire," and the bottom part, a stylization of 人, represents a person, signifying "function." The function of fire is light. In Japan, the statues of Amitabha Buddha have a round glowing sphere behind him to symbolize the infinite light and life he radiates. In Japanese, a supreme being is *gokō ga sasu* (後光が差す) or "someone who shines with radiant light from behind."

Kanji Facts

There are currently 1,945 officially approved kanji. Used especially by general-interest newspapers and magazines, these are called the Jōyō Kanji, or "Kanji for Everyday Use."

The Way of Nature

光　　光　　光　　光

Formal　　　　Modern　　　　Flowing　　　　Stylish

The Way of Nature

This ideogram is made of 門, which means "gate," and 音, which means "sound" but also expresses the onyomi pronunciation *an*. The gate symbolizes a closed-off place where only the faintest sounds of the world can be heard.

闇　闇　闇　闇

Formal　　　Modern　　　Flowing　　　Stylish

蓮華

The Way of Nature

The kanji 蓮 (*ren*) means "the lotus" and 華 (*ge*) means "flower." In Buddhism, the lotus symbolizes the Pure Land of Heaven. This symbol came from the *Saddharmapundrika Sutra*. *Saddharma* means "the right laws of the universe." *Pundrika* refers to the lotus flower. Born in a muddy marsh, the lotus grows to enormous beauty and rises above its humble origins. Like it, humans can rise above their circumstances and transform their lives without being pulled into the swamp of earthly desires and suffering. In Japan, the *Lotus Sutra* is known as 妙法蓮華経 (*Myōhō Renge Kyō*).

蓮華   蓮華   蓮華   蓮華

Formal   Modern   Flowing   Stylish

The Way of Nature

The left side of this kanji means "animal," and the right side express-es the onyomi pronunciation *byo*. A familiar figurine in Japanese business storefronts is the *maneki-neko*, or "beckoning cat" with one paw raised in welcome to customers (and their money). This lucky charm originated in seventeenth-century Edo (present-day Tokyo), when a poor old woman had to abandon her beloved cat because she could no longer afford to feed it. One night, her cat came to her in a dream and told her to make a cat doll. She modeled it after him. The dolls became very popular, and the poor old woman became rich. Today the *maneki-neko* is considered a symbol of prosperity and wealth.

猫 猫 猫 猫

Since ancient times, hawks have been considered the most majestic and noble birds in Japan. Many samurai family crests incorporated the shapes of hawk feathers in their design, and real hawk feathers were used for arrow flights. One popular Japanese proverb says, "A wise hawk hides his claws" (能ある鷹は爪を隠す: *nō aru taka wa tsume wo kakusu*), or, in other words, "talented people never reveal their skills." The lower element 鳥 represents a bird with long feathers. The top part expresses the *onyomi* pronunciation ō or yō.

The Way of Nature

鷹 鷹 鷹 鷹

Formal   Modern   Flowing   Stylish   101

The Way of Nature

The left side of this character is the radical element for "animal," and the right side expresses the onyomi pronunciation *ro*. Wolves have long been revered as gods or as messengers of the Mountain God. In fact, the pronunciation of "wolf" (狼) and "Great God" (大神) is the same: *ōkami*.

Kanji Facts

Kanji are composed of a number of strokes in a fixed sequence. Some kanji have only a single stroke, and some have as many as thirty-three.

狼　　狼　　狼　　狼

　　Formal　　　　Modern　　　　Flowing　　　　Stylish

The upper part 雨 of this character means "rain." In ancient times, three 田 symbols, pronounced *"den,"* were at the bottom of the kanji, symbolizing the sound of a great thunderclap. The Thunder God is a muscular, larger-than-life demon with an assortment of drums on his back to help him make this enormous sound. See also RAIN, THUNDER GOD.

The Way of Nature

The Way of Nature

This character is made of three trees (木), shown with strong trunks and spreading branches. 森 thus symbolizes a place where there are many trees, such as a forest. In Japanese, a mountain echo is called *kodama* (木霊), which means "tree spirit." Ancient Japanese believed that the spirits who live in trees respond to the human voice.

Kanji Facts

In Japan, you'll often see a kanji with its reading spelled out beside it in small syllabic characters called *furigana*. These are to help readers, especially young people, with pronunciation.

Formal   Modern   Flowing   Stylish

The Way
of the Spirit

The Way of the Spirit

The right side 首 of this character is the kanji for "neck," which symbolizes the top of the head, the highest place in the body. It also means "goal." The trailing element on the left means "to go to." The ideogram 道 (*michi* in Japanese or *tao* in Chinese) means "the Way" or "the path," the central concept in Taoism. Lao-tzu interpreted the Tao as the basic law of the universe, saying, "道 (the Way) is like a vessel. Even when emptied over and over again, it doesn't need to be full. New water always springs forth, and it is bottomless. It is like the origin of everything." Many martial arts and artistic disciplines apply the kanji 道 (usually read *dō* when used in a compound) to their names to indicate that they are fundamentally concerned with spiritual growth: *aikidō*, *shodō* (calligraphy), *kadō* (flower arrangement, *sadō* (tea ceremony), and so on. See also BUSHIDŌ, GAY.

道　　道　　道　　道

Formal　　　　Modern　　　　Flowing　　　　Stylish

The ideogram 無 (*mu*) represents a very profound Zen expression meaning "nothingness," "the void," and "the original cosmos beyond existence or nonexistence." In the ninth century, the Chinese priest Jōshū was asked the following Zen koan by another priest: "Does a dog have Buddha nature (仏性)?" Jōshū's answer was "無." In Buddhism, every being in this world has Buddha nature. Jōshū's answer essentially means, "When we reach the state of 無, it doesn't matter." See also BUDDHA NATURE, INVINCIBLE.

The Way of the Spirit

Formal   Modern   Flowing   Stylish

仏 陀

When Buddhism came to China from India in the first century A.D., the Chinese represented its concepts with ideograms chosen for the similarity of their pronunciations to the imported Sanskrit words. The name "Buddha" comes from the Sanskrit word *budh,* which means "to enlighten" or "to know," but the original Chinese meaning of this kanji was "to bear a resemblance to someone else." The pronunciation of 仏 in Japanese is *butsu*; the ideogram is often used by itself to mean "Buddha" or to indicate some connection to Buddhism.

仏
陀

仏
陀

仏
陀

仏
陀

Formal

Modern

Flowing

Stylish

覚 者

This compound is the Chinese translation of the word "Buddha," which " in Sanskrit means "fully awakened one." The first kanji 覚 (*kaku*) means "to awaken," and 者 (*sha* or *ja*) means "person." The original ideogram of 覚 was the more complex 覺, whose crosses at the top express the pronunciation *kaku* and symbolize arms reaching out to pass down knowledge. The lower part 見 means "to look at," "to know," "to remember," and "to awaken." Gautama Siddhartha (Buddha's given name) was the first "fully awakened one," an enlightened being who transcended his earthly body. We generally think of him as "the Buddha," though many other enlightened beings such as Amitabha Buddha and Maha Vairocana Buddha appeared after his death.

The Way of the Spirit

覚者 覚者 覚者 覚者

Formal   Modern   Flowing   Stylish

Bodhisattva

菩薩

The word "bodhisattva" comes from the Sanskrit word *bodhi*. A *bodhi* is someone who has undergone intense spiritual training to reach a state of enlightenment and who is committed to helping others alleviate suffering. Dharmakara Bodhisattva (法蔵菩薩), who later became Amitabha Buddha, is a familiar example. When he became a bodhisattva he vowed, "I cannot become a Buddha until all beings in this world are saved."

The Way of the Spirit

菩薩　菩薩　菩薩　菩薩

Formal　Modern　Flowing　Stylish

慈　悲

Compassion is the highest ethical precept of Buddhism. The compound 慈悲 (*jihi*) is the Chinese translation of the Sanskrit terms *maitri* ("give joy") and *karuna* ("relieve suffering"). The first kanji 慈 (*ji*) means "to love" and "mercy"; it combines a top element 茲, which expresses the pronunciation *ji* and means "to grow," and a bottom element 心, which means "heart." The kanji 悲 means "to feel sadness" and "sympathy" and is made of a top element 非, which means "to separate into left and right," and again of 心, "heart." Thus this kanji compound expresses the belief that when you love you feel someone else's sadness, and relieve their suffering through empathy. Such is the nature of compassion. There is no separation between ourselves and others, and Buddha is compassionate to all beings.

The Way of the Spirit

慈悲　慈悲　慈悲　慈悲

観 音 菩 薩

The Way of the Spirit

Kannon is the Buddhist goddess of mercy and compassion. Her Indian name Avalokitesvara comes from the Sanskrit *avalokita* ("to see") and *isvara* ("higher power" or "lord"). In the fourth century A.D. her name was misspelled in China as Avalokitasvara and translated into 観音, pronounced "Kannon." 観 (*Kan*) means "to observe" and 音 (*on*) means "sound"; thus the literal meaning is "to observe sound" or "she who hears the cries of the world." In the eighth century the name Kannon was correctly retranslated as 観自在菩薩 or "Kanjizai Bosatsu," that is, "one who observes freely." By that time, however, the name Kannon had already taken hold. See also BODHISATTVA.

観
音
菩
薩

観
音
菩
薩

観
音
菩
薩

観
音
菩
薩

Formal

Modern

Flowing

Stylish

阿弥陀仏

Amida Buddha is the Buddha that lives in the Pure Land (Heaven) and saves those who seek salvation. The word 阿弥陀 (*amida*) is derived from the sound of the Sanskrit names Amitabha, which means "infinite light" (無量光: *muryokō*), and Amitayum, which means "infinite life" (無量寿: *muryoju*).

The Way of the Spirit

阿弥陀仏　　阿弥陀仏　　阿弥陀仏　　阿弥陀仏

Formal	Modern	Flowing	Stylish	

大 日 如 来

The kanji 大 (*dai*) means "big" or "great," and 日 (*nichi*) means "the sun" and "light." 大日 literally means "big light" and is the translation of Maha Vairocana, which means "great illumination" in Sanskrit. The kanji *nyo* (如) means "absolute truth," and in this case *rai* (来) means "to come." The compound 如来 thus means "someone coming from the truth," such as a Buddha. In Tantric Buddhism, known in Japanese as Mikkyō (密教), the Buddha named Maha Vairocana is the absolute immortal Buddha. Even Gautama Buddha is a reincarnation of his spirit.

大
日
如
来

大
日
如
来

大
日
如
来

大
日
如
来

瑜 伽

The kanji 瑜 means "a type of jade"; the element 王 on the left means "jewelry," and the radical on the right expresses the pronunciation *yu*. The kanji 伽 is used to express the Sanskrit pronunciation *ga* or *ka*. Yoga in Buddhism is different from the yoga that is currently practiced in most yoga studios, which emphasizes postures, breathing, chanting, and meditation. In Buddhism, *yuga* is taking care of the mind, body, and spirit through *zazen*-style sitting, breathing, and meditation. Modern "yoga" is usually written with the katakana phonetic characters ヨガ.

The Way of the Spirit

瑜
伽

瑜
伽

瑜
伽

瑜
伽

解 脱

The Way of the Spirit

The first character 解 means "unbind" and is made of the elements "horn" (角), "sword" (刀), and "ox" (牛). Its original meaning was "to cut the ox," that is, to separate the meat from the bone. The second character 脱 means "to cast off"; the radical on the left means "body," and that on the right means "separate." *Gedatsu*, a Buddhist term that means "to cut the binds of desire, worry, and suffering to attain enlightenment," is a translation of the Sanskrit *vimukti*, which means "total liberation." Rinzai, a ninth-century Zen priest, said, "When you meet the Buddha, kill the Buddha. When you meet your ancestors, kill your ancestors. When you meet an *arhat* [an enlightened monk] kill the *arhat*. Then, you will finally be liberated (解脱)." See also INDEPENDENCE.

解
脱

解
脱

解
脱

解
脱

Formal

Modern

Flowing

Stylish

The Way of the Spirit

The ideogram 空 (*kū*) means "emptiness" and is the Chinese translation of the Sanskrit term *sunyata* or "void." Its antonym is 色 (*shiki*), meaning "all that has form." 空 is made of "hole" (穴) and the element 工, which expresses the pronunciation *kū*. A famous phrase in the *Parajaparmita Sutra* says 色即是空 (*shiki soku ze kū*: "form is emptiness") and 空即是色 (*kū soku ze shiki*: "emptiness is form"). The kanji 空 can also be pronounced *kara*, as in the martial art 空手 (*karate*), whose literal meaning is "empty hand."

空   空   空   空

Formal   Modern   Flowing   Stylish

正業

The Way of the Spirit

The first kanji 正 (*shō*) means "good," "correct," or "just." The original meaning of the second kanji 業 (*gō*) is "skill" and "work," but when Buddhism came to China this kanji was used to translate the Sanskrit term *karma*, the past-life deeds or actions that are the determinants of one's current existence. On its own, the ideogram 業 for *karma* generally means "bad karma" in Japanese, since if our past life had been virtuous we would be in the Pure Land instead of being reborn into human form. Therefore, we combine the two ideograms to form 正業 (*shōgō*) or "good karma."

正業　正業　正業　正業

Formal　　　　*Modern*　　　　*Flowing*　　　　*Stylish*

般若

This term is derived from the Sanskrit *paraja*, which means "wisdom." In Buddhism, 般若 (*han-nya*) means "the wisdom to determine right action from wrong." In Japanese, 般若 has another interesting meaning as well: "she-devil." History has it that the priest named Hannyabō (般若坊) made a frightening mask of a female demon for a Noh play, and ever since that time the she-devils in Japan have been known as *hannya*.

Kanji Facts

In the Japanese translation of the Harry Potter books, the kanji for "dragon" (*ryū* or *tatsu*) is used, but the pronunciation *doragon* ("dragon") is written in syllables above the character.

The Way of the Spirit

般若   般若   般若   般若

涅槃

The Way of the Spirit

The two ideograms 涅槃 represent the Sanskrit word *nirvana*. The original meaning of *nirvana* was "to blow off" the fire of earthly cravings, reaching an ideal state of complete freedom from desire, worry, and suffering. Someone who has reached *nirvana* breaks the cycle of *karma* and will no longer be incarnated in earthly form. Though the day Buddha reached *nirvana* is unknown, February 15 is honored as Buddha's death day. On that day, memorial ceremonies called *nehan-e* (涅槃会) are held in temples throughout Japan, Korea, and China. See also FLOWER, HEART.

涅槃   涅槃   涅槃   涅槃

達磨

Daruma was the founder of the Zen sect of Buddhism. His Chinese name is 菩提達磨 (Bo-dai-daru-ma), which is derived from his original Sanskrit name, Bodhidharma. *Bodhi* means "to be awakened," and *dharma* means "the laws of this earth." Daruma was born a privileged Brahmin in southern India in the fifth century A.D. But after studying Buddhism he left his wife and child in India and journeyed to China, where he entered a Shaolin temple and sat facing a wall in meditation, it is said, for nine years. In Japan, Daruma is depicted as a round ball with a face but without arms or legs, since the years he devoted to seated meditation caused his physical body to atrophy and dematerialize.

The Way of the Spirit

達磨 達磨 達磨 達磨

The Way of the Spirit

The word "Zen" (禅) comes from the Buddhist term 禅那 (*zenna*), the Chinese pronunciation of the Sanskrit term *dhyana*, which means "concentration" as a means of awakening consciousness—one of the eight limbs of yogic practice as stated in the *Yoga Sutra*. Zen is widely known as a type of Buddhist practice in which meditation serves as the gateway to liberation. Zen came to Japan from China in the twelfth century and was the most popular religion of the samurai class in medieval times. It has profoundly influenced almost all Japanese artistic, martial, and spiritual practices.

禅　禅　禅　禅

Formal　　　　　Modern　　　　　Flowing　　　　　Stylish

仏性

The kanji compound 仏性 (*busshō*) represents the Sanskrit term *budhata*, which means "Buddha nature." The first kanji 仏 (*butsu*) means "the Buddha," and 性 (*shō*) means "nature" or "essence." *The Mahaparinibbanasuttanta*, the sacred Buddhist text that documents the days before and after the Buddha's death, quotes Buddha: "Every being in this world has Buddha nature." Even dogs, cats, insects, and plants have Buddha nature, the ability to attain enlightenment and to be awakened. The main concept of Buddhism, often overlooked, is that nirvana is available to all. See also NOTHINGNESS.

The Way of the Spirit

仏性　仏性　仏性　仏性

| Formal | Modern | Flowing | Stylish | 123 |

咒術

The first kanji 咒 (*ju*) means "to charm" or "to conjure." 術 means "skill." The upper part of 咒 has two "mouth" (口) elements; the bottom part (几) means "desk" and here symbolizes an altar. The kanji thus literally means "to open the mouth, casting a spell at an altar." The ancient Japanese magician Onyoji used spirits called 式神 (*shikigami*) to cast his powerful spells. *Shikigami* usually took the form of paper dolls or figures drawn on paper. Once a spirit was possessed by Onyoji, it came to life. This legend may in fact be the origin of the cartoon characters in the hugely popular *Pokémon* series.

咒術 咒術 咒術 咒術

Formal   Modern   Flowing   Stylish

The Way of the Spirit

The Way of the Spirit

In China, the kanji 鬼 originally meant "soul" or "departed spirit," but in Japanese it symbolizes a muscle-bound demon with red or blue skin and two horns growing from its head. Japanese folklorists believe the term might have first been used to describe the indigenous Japanese people, or Emishi, who fought against the emperor's occupying army from the third to eighth centuries. The emperor's troops, who encountered the bitter resistance of the Emishi as they struggled to keep their land, called them *oni* or "demons." Nowadays, Japanese sometimes use 鬼 in a more positive way; for example, someone who works with near-inhuman energy is a 仕事の鬼 (*shigoto no oni*: literally, a "demon worker").

鬼　鬼　鬼　鬼

Formal　　　　Modern　　　　Flowing　　　　Stylish

The Way of the Spirit

The right part of this ideogram contains 鬼 (*oni:* "demon"), whose original Chinese meaning is "soul" or "departed spirit," The left part 云 signifies a cloud and expresses the pronunciation *kon*. The kanji thus represents the idea that the souls of the dead rise up to the clouds. The ancient Japanese pronounced this ideogram *tama*, referring to the life-force energy that enters the body, guiding the heart and mind. Death occurs when the soul (now pronounced *tamashii*) leaves the physical body. In Japan, the word *tamashii* can refer to the soul of either the living or the dead. See also DEMON.

Kanji Facts

Calligraphy, or *shodô*, is the art of writing beautiful kanji. It is a popular hobby in Japan, learned in school and practiced by everyone from housewives to Zen priests.

Formal   Modern   Flowing   Stylish

The first kanji 言 (*koto*) means "word." 霊 (*Dama*)—made of the elements 雨 ("rain") and 巫 ("shaman")—in ancient China meant "magical sky-spirits" but now means "departed spirit" in Japanese and is usually pronounced *rei. Kotodama* reflects the ancient animistic concept that god's magical power exists in words. The ancient Japanese believed that spirit exists in everything in this world—even in stone and sand—and that using words with respect, thereby honoring the objects they describe, would bring happiness. See also RAIN.

The Way of the Spirit

Formal   Modern   Flowing   Stylish

The Way of the Spirit

The main part of this kanji is made up of 目 for "eye" and 夕 for "night." What is seen in the night are dreams. In Chinese and Japanese, the ideogram for "dream" also has the nuance of "transience" or "fragility." The ancient Chinese legend of the "The Kantan Dream" tells of a young man who sets out for the capital to make his fortune, stopping at a small town called Kantan along the way and falling asleep at a station house. As he sleeps, he dreams of becoming the king in the capital. In his dream, he has become old, very sick, and near death. When he awakens, he realizes that he has dreamed his whole life away. Now aware that life is fleeting, he returns to his hometown, where he spends the rest of his life living humbly and satisfied.

Formal   Modern   Flowing   Stylish

At the center of this kanji is 心, the ideogram for "heart." Above the heart is the kanji for "breath," and below the heart is the kanji for "graceful movement." Love breathes mercy into the heart, bringing grace into the body and transforming us. This ideogram was originally made of 心 plus 旡, which meant "feeding a guest." The original Chinese meaning was more "hospitality of the heart," or "to show mercy." In Japan, the kanji was first used to express the feeling of liking, admiring, and appreciating things like nature or art, but when Christianity arrived in the middle of the nineteenth century, 愛 (*ai*) began to take on the European meaning of "love." See also HEART.

The Way of the Spirit

永 劫

The first kanji 永 *(ei)* means "a long time." It depicts many streams branching out from a river and flowing onward; the two strokes on the sides represent foam and ripples, perhaps symbolizing the ebb and flow of time. The kanji 劫 *(gō)* comes from 劫波 *(kōha)*, the Chinese term for the Sanskrit *kalpa*, which in ancient India was considered the longest possible stretch of time, defined as the amount of time it takes for the highest mountain to be completely worn away by the touch of the soft sleeve of a celestial nymph who comes down from the heavens every hundred years. See also WATER.

永 劫　　永 劫　　永 劫　　永 劫

Formal　　　　Modern　　　　Flowing　　　　Stylish

悟 り

The word 悟り (*satori*) means "to understand the truth and be liberated from earthy desires and suffering" and is often translated by the single word "enlightenment." It uses the Chinese character 悟 (*sato*), meaning "enlightenment," followed by the Japanese phonetic character り (*ri*) to create a Japanese translation of the term 解脱 (*gedatsu*), which itself was the Chinese rendering of the Sanskrit *vimukti* ("total liberation"). Musō Soseki, the medieval Japanese Zen poet/priest, wrote, "When one understands the truth and achieves enlightenment, there is no difference between life and death." To achieve *satori* means to reach the realm of 無 (*mu*) or nothingness. See also LIBERATION, NOTHINGNESS.

The Way of the Spirit

悟 り

悟 り

悟 り

悟 り

地 獄

This kanji compound combines 地 (*ji*: "ground") and 獄 (*goku*: "prison"); an "underground prison" is an apt image of hell. In Japan, there are believed to be several kinds of hell: (1) the hell where people are forced to kill each other, (2) the hell where people are tied down with chains of fire, (3) the hell where people are crushed by iron mountains, (4) the hell of boiled water, (5) the hell where people's tongues are pulled out by demons, (6) the hell of fire, (7) the hell of the hottest fire, (8) the hell of sword mountain, and (9) the hell of the boiling pond. The King of Hell, Enma Daiō (閻魔大王), determines which hell people will be sent to according to their karmic debts.

地 地 地 地
獄 獄 獄 獄

Formal   Modern   Flowing   Stylish

This is the Buddhist term for Heaven or Paradise, composed of the characters 浄 (*jō*: "pure") and 土 (*do*: "land"). In East Asia, the Pure Land was believed to exist to the west of India. The medieval Japanese poet Saigyō (西行) named himself after this belief, since 西 (*sai*) means "west" and 行 (*gyō*) means "to go": literally, "go toward the west and guide the people to the Pure Land." Another word for Heaven is 天国 (*tengoku*). 天 (*Ten*) means "sky," and depicts a person (人) standing under the sky. 国 (*Koku*) means "country." 天国 is frequently used to express the Christian notion of Heaven.

The Way of the Spirit

浄土   浄土   浄土   浄土

The aesthetic and literary quality known as 侘 (*wabi*) is the main characteristic of the Japanese tea ceremony, sometimes called *wabi-cha* (侘茶), that was founded by Murata Jukō in the 1400s and popularized by the teamaster Sen-no-Rikyu in the next century. *Wabi-cha* symbolizes a way of life embodied in the tea ceremony itself, which is enjoyed in a small, rustic, natural, uncluttered haven outside of space and time. The ideal of *wabi* embraces a lifestyle of simplicity, modesty, and humility, living close to nature, unencumbered and serene.

侘　　侘　　侘　　侘

The aesthetic and literary quality known as 寂 (*sabi*) is the main feature of the haiku of Bashō, Japan's most famous poet. The original meaning of *sabi* suggests a scene that is old, quiet, and lonely, a circumstance reflected in the lifestyle of the wandering haiku poet who embraces the transience of life. Life is impermanent, imperfect, and incomplete. People and things die, get old, rust, fade, fall apart, break. This is their beauty and their sadness, part of the endless cycle of existence. The following haiku embodies Bashō's sense of *sabi*:

> The sick goose flies down / in the cold night, taking sleep / along the journey.

寂 寂 寂 寂

精 神

  This word combines 精 (*sei*), meaning "pure," "superior," or "profound," with 神 (*shin*), meaning "mind" or "soul." The 米 radical on the left side of 精 means "rice"; its original meaning was "polished rice becomes pure." The kanji 神 combines 礻, which symbolizes god or the divine, and 申, which originally symbolized a thunderbolt and later meant "to give orders." Chinese mythology says that we enter the world and receive our soul at birth, which becomes an active "spirit" at death. It is believed that these spirits send us "signs" from the netherworld to guide us in life. See also ENERGY.

精
神

精
神

精
神

精
神

Formal   Modern   Flowing   Stylish

The Animals of the Twelve Zodiac Signs

十二支

Around 2000 B.C., the ancient Chinese discovered that Jupiter—which they considered the most auspicious planet—orbited the earth every twelve years. The Chinese astronomers divided the orbit into twelve directions and gave each direction a different name. These names were used merely to indicate the year and Jupiter's position, like the points on a compass. Later, around 100 B.C., the name of an animal was assigned to each of the twelve directions, perhaps to help people remember their birth years. Over time, persons born in a particular year were thought to possess qualities of that year's animal, a belief that continues to this day. The cycle of twelve animals begins again every twelve years. Each year is represented by two kanji, and both are listed here: the first is the animal assigned to the year, and the second is the original Chinese character for the "compass point."

Rat

nezumi

鼠

子

This ideogram depicts a rat—the top symbolizes its head and teeth. In Japan, a white rat is considered a messenger of the God of Wealth, Daikokuten, and is a harbinger of prosperity and success in business.

Year of the Rat

shi, ne

The original Chinese ideogram—made up of 了 (*ryō*) or "end," and 一 (*ichi*), meaning "one" or "the first"—symbolizes a seed from which everything on earth is born. The combination of these elements expresses the philosophy that the end of something is the beginning of something else. The direction in the cycle is North. The time is around 12:00 P.M. People born in the Year of the Rat are considered hard workers and are known for their frugality and wealth. These perfectionists are also skilled at charming others and are usually quite successful. Birth years: 1900, 1912, 1924, 1936, 1948, 1960, 1972, 1984, 1996, 2008.

Ox

ushi

牛

丑

This figure depicts an ox. The upper horizontal bar represents the horns. In Asia, the ox and cow are used for cultivation and transporting goods. Their quiet, hard-working nature epitomizes patience and perseverance.

Year of the Ox

chū, ushi

The original Chinese ideogram depicts a root with a seed emerging from it; the root is tangled underground, waiting for spring to come. Its original meaning was "to tie the wrists," but it later came to just mean "tie." The direction in the cycle is North-northeast. The time is around 2:00 A.M. Those born in the Year of the Ox are considered patient, steadfast in their belief in themselves, and able to inspire confidence in others. Ox people don't give up on their dreams. Birth years: 1901, 1913, 1925, 1937, 1949, 1961, 1973, 1985, 1997, 2009.

Tiger

tora

虎

寅

This kanji depicts a tiger with an open mouth, roaring. In ancient times, tigers inhabited many Asian countries. Since there were no lions, people considered the tiger the strongest animal in the jungle. In Japan, a strong and brave general is called a "Tiger General" or 虎将 (*koshō*).

Year of the Tiger

in, tora

The original Chinese ideogram of the kanji was made up of 虫 ("insect") and 寅 (the sound *in*). Just as an insect moves almost imperceptibly across the earth, sprouts appear, shooting up from the soil. The direction in the cycle is East-northeast. The time is around 4:00 A.M. The tiger represents a prudent person. Those born in the Year of the Tiger are believed to possess fierce power and can often have issues with authority. But they are also courageous, sensitive, deep-thinking, and sympathetic to others. Birth years: 1902, 1914, 1926, 1938, 1950, 1962, 1974, 1986, 1998, 2010.

Rabbit

usagi

This ideogram depicts a rabbit; the curved line at the top symbolizes its ears. Japanese believe that a rabbit makes rice cakes on the moon. How did he get there? An ancient Indian legend tells of a rabbit who met a weary old traveler on the road. The rabbit wanted to help the traveler but couldn't find any food, so it made a fire and threw its body onto the flames. The traveler turned out to be the Lord of Heaven, who was so impressed that he took the spirit of the rabbit with him to the moon.

Year of the Rabbit

bō, u

The original Chinese ideogram depicts a plant that has begun to grow. All living things break ground when they mature. The direction in the cycle is East. The time is around 6:00 A.M. Those born in the Year of the Rabbit are considered articulate, talented, and ambitious. They are virtuous and admired by others. Birth years: 1903, 1915, 1927, 1939, 1951, 1963, 1975, 1987, 1999, 2011.

Dragon

ryū

This ideogram depicts the profile of a dragon, with its scaly, curved body and long tail. The Japanese believe that the dragon causes rain and thunder; a tornado is called a "coiled dragon" or 龍巻 (*tatsumaki*) because according to legend a dragon flies up to the sky in a funnel-shaped wind.

Year of the Dragon

shin, tatsu

The original Chinese ideogram symbolizes the understanding that every living thing grows to maturity in the spring. The direction in the cycle is East-southeast. The time is around 8:00 A.M. The dragon represents the power to lift the sky. It symbolizes superiority. Those born in the Year of the Dragon are energetic, excitable, brave, and honest. The dragon is also considered the most eccentric sign in the Chinese Zodiac. Birth years: 1904, 1916, 1928, 1940, 1952, 1964, 1976, 1988, 2000, 2012.

Snake

hebi

The element on the left originally meant a large-headed snake and later became the character 虫 (*mushi*) for "insect." The Chinese classified anything other than human beings, four-legged beasts, fish, birds, and crustaceans as insects. That's why the ideograms for octopus (*tako*: 蛸), lizard (*tokage*: 蜥蜴), and frog (*kaeru*: 蛙) contain the "insect" kanji 虫. The snake is also considered a messenger of the gods.

Year of the Snake

shi, mi

The original Chinese ideogram symbolizes the time of year when daylight lasts the longest. The direction in the cycle is South-southeast. The time is around 10:00 A.M. Those born in the year of the snake possess great inner wisdom and depth. Although outwardly calm and quiet, they are inwardly fiery and passionate. They are self-sufficient, but also very sympathetic to those in need. Birth years: 1905, 1917, 1929, 1941, 1953, 1965, 1977, 1989, 2001, 2013.

馬

午

羊

未

猿

申

Horse

uma

This ideogram depicts a galloping horse, its mane waving in the wind. Japanese used to bring real horses to shrines to make their devotions, and from this derives the custom of visiting a shrine to write your wish on a small wooden placard called an 絵馬 *(ema: "horse picture")*: the kanji 絵 *(e)* means "picture." Each placard corresponds to a particular animal among the twelve in the zodiac.

Year of the Horse

go, uma

The original Chinese ideogram expresses the balance of light and dark forces. The "darkness" 陰 *(yin)* appears to be pushing away the "light" 陽 *(yang)*, symbolizing June, the month of the summer solstice when the days start to shorten. The direction in the cycle is South. The time is around 12:00 A.M. Those born in the Year of the Horse move at a fast pace. They are cheerful, popular, perceptive people who are often skilled with their hands. Birth years: 1906, 1918 1930, 1942, 1954, 1966, 1978, 1990, 2002, 2014.

Sheep/Ram

hitsuji

This kanji depicts a sheep, with the two spikes on top representing the horns. In China, sheep used to be revered for their docility and were offered to the gods. Therefore, this ideogram also means "goodness."

Year of the Ram

mi, hitsuji

The original Chinese ideogram depicts the growth of leaves and branches from a stem. It symbolizes the time when fruit ripens, bursting with flavor. The direction in the cycle is South-southwest. The time is around 2:00 P.M. Those born in the Year of the Sheep are considered gentle, warm-hearted, and compassionate. Though some are shy, many are elegant and talented in the arts. Birth years: 1907, 1919, 1931, 1943, 1955, 1967, 1979, 1991, 2003, 2015.

Monkey

saru

This ideogram is made from the "animal" radical on the left and an element expressing the onyomi pronunciation *en*. Monkeys are considered messengers of god and protective spirits. In medieval times, samurai kept monkeys in their stables to shield their horses from evil.

Year of the Monkey

shin, saru

The original Chinese ideogram means "to come to complete maturity in autumn." Perhaps that is why the pronunciation *shin* for "monkey" is the same as that of the kanji 身, meaning "body," which originally symbolized a pregnant woman and literally meant "bearing fruit." The direction in the cycle is West-southwest. The time is around 4:00 P.M. Those born in the Year of the Monkey are considered inventive, skillful, and strong willed. They are unique, determined people who can accomplish almost any goal. The Chinese consider them the "erratic geniuses" of the Zodiac cycle. Birth years: 1908, 1920, 1932, 1944, 1956, 1968, 1980, 1992, 2004, 2016.

馬 午
馬 午
馬 午
馬

羊 未
羊 未
羊 未
羊 未

猿 申
猿 申
猿 申
猿

鶏 酉

Rooster
niwatori

The element 鳥 (*tori*) on the right side of this kanji depicts a bird with long feathers. The left side expresses the pronunciation *kei*. Buddhist temples prohibited animals on their grounds, with one exception: roosters—invaluable to Buddhist priests for helping them wake up on time for their meditation and rituals.

Year of the Cock/Rooster
yū, tori

The original Chinese ideogram depicts a bottle of spirits. It is symbolic of the time of maturity, the ripening of autumn. The direction in the cycle is West. The time is around 6:00 P.M. Those born in the Year of the Rooster are deep thinking and capable. Considered talented and outspoken, they like to keep busy and be sociable, although they also enjoy being alone. Birth years: 1909, 1921 1933, 1945, 1957, 1969, 1981, 1993, 2005, 2017.

鶏 鶏 鶏 鶏   酉 酉 酉 酉

犬 戌

Dog
inu

This kanji depicts the profile of a walking dog, with the curved stroke at the top right representing an ear. Dogs are revered in Japan for their loyalty. In downtown Tokyo, there is the statue of an Akita dog named Hachiko, who lived in the 1930s and walked his master to the train station in Shibuya every day, waiting there faithfully for his return from work. Even after his owner's death, Hachiko kept up his daily vigil at the station until he too died eight years later. People were so impressed that they built a statue in Hachiko's honor.

Year of the Dog
jutsu, inu

The original Chinese ideogram symbolizes the time when leaves and grass wither, but this kanji has the same meaning as 恤 (*jutsu*), or "mercy." In the cycle of existence, there is a time for everything, even death, which should be accepted, even embraced. The direction in the cycle is West-northwest. The time is 8:00 P.M. Those born in the Year of the Dog have a strong sense of justice, honesty, privacy, honor, and loyalty. Birth years: 1910, 1922 1934, 1946, 1958, 1970, 1982, 1994, 2006, 2018.

犬 犬 犬   戌 戌 戌

猪 亥

Wild Boar
inoshishi

Pigs were kept as livestock in Japan until the sixth century, when Buddhism began to exert a strong influence. Buddhist doctrine prohibited the eating of animals, so people stopped raising pigs for consumption. However, some did continue to hunt wild boar, or 猪 (*inoshishi*). The kanji for "pig" thus came to be synonymous with "wild boar." Pigs were not kept as livestock in Japan again until the mid-nineteenth century. In Japan today, the kanji 豚 (*buta*) is used for "pig."

Year of the Pig
gai, i

The original Chinese ideogram means "core" or "center" and is symbolic of the fact that the essence of life is located at the core within. The direction in the cycle is North-northwest. The time is 10:00 P.M. Those born in the Year of the Pig are strong willed and have great fortitude. They enjoy learning and acquiring knowledge, and they are chivalrous and kind to their loved ones. Birth years: 1911, 1923, 1935, 1947, 1959, 1971, 1983, 1995, 2007, 2019.

猪 猪 猪   亥 亥 亥

Bibliography

The following references were consulted in the preparation of this book:

Bukkyōjiten (Buddhism Dictionary). Tokyo: Iwanami Shoten, 2002.

Chūgoku no Shisō (Chinese Thought). Tokyo: Tokuma Shoten, 1973.

Fukutake Kanwajiten (Fukutake Kanji Dictionary). Tokyo: Fukutake Shoten, 1987.

Iwanami Kokugojiten (Iwanami Japanese Dictionary). Tokyo: Iwanami Shoten, 1974.

Kamo-no-Chōmei, *Hojoki: Visions of a Torn World*. Translated by Yasuhiko Moriguchi and David Jenkins. Berkeley: Stone Bridge Press, 1996.

Kanno, Michiaki. *Jigen* (The Origin of Kanji). Tokyo: Kadokawa Shoten, 1962.

Kogojiten (Archaic Japanese Words Dictionary). Tokyo: Kadokawa Shoten, 1974.

Kojien (Kojien Japanese Dictionary). Tokyo: Iwanami Shoten, 1998.

Minakata Kumakusu Senshū (Selected Works of Kumakusu Minakata). Tokyo: Heibon Sha, 1984.

Nihon Shijin Zenshū (Collected Works of Japanese Poets). Tokyo: Shinchō Sha, 1973.

Sekai no Meicho (World Classic Books) Tokyo: Chuōkōron Sha, 1968.

Shinchō Koten Shūsei (Collected Series of Japanese Classics). Tokyo: Shinchō Sha, 1982.

Shinsen Kanwajiten (New Selected Kanji Dictionary) Tokyo: Shōgakukan, 1970.

Shirakawa, Shizuka. *Jitō* (The Kanji Dictionary). Tokyo: Heibon Sha, 1994.

Yanagida Kunio Zenshū (Collected Works of Kunio Yanagida). Tokyo: Chikuma Shobō, 1990.

And online at:

www.c-c-c.org/chineseculture/zodiac/zodiac.html: Chinese Culture Center's Zodiac page

www.Japan-Guide.com: Schauwecker's Guide to Japan

www.kanjigraphy.com: Royalty-Free Calligraphy Images

www.zenkou.com: Quotes, Virtues, and Japanese kanji

Two recommended books for kanji students are:

Henshall, Kenneth. *A Guide to Remembering Japanese Characters*. Tokyo: Tuttle, 1995.

Rowley, Michael. *Kanji Pict-o-Graphix: Over 1,000 Japanese Kanji and Kana Mnemonics*. Berkeley: Stone Bridge Press, 1992.

Index